CONVICTING AVERY

CONVICTING AVERY

THE BIZARRE LAWS AND BROKEN SYSTEM BEHIND *MAKING A MURDERER*

MICHAEL D. CICCHINI

COMPLETELY UNAUTHORIZED

Prometheus Books

59 John Glenn Drive
Amherst, New York 14228

Published 2017 by Prometheus Books

Cover image © AP Images
Cover design by Nicole Sommer-Lecht
Cover design © Prometheus Books

Inquiries should be addressed to
Prometheus Books
59 John Glenn Drive
Amherst, New York 14228
VOICE: 716–691–0133
FAX: 716–691–0137
WWW.PROMETHEUSBOOKS.COM

21 20 19 18 17   5 4 3 2 1

Library of Congress Cataloging-in-Publication Data

Names: Cicchini, Michael D., 1967- author.
Title: Convicting Avery : the bizarre laws and broken system behind "making a murderer" / Michael Cicchini.
Description: Amherst, New York : Prometheus Books, 2017.
Identifiers: LCCN 2016036579 (print) | LCCN 2016036649 (ebook) | ISBN 9781633882553 (paperback) | ISBN 9781633882560 (ebook)
Subjects: LCSH: Avery, Steven—Trials, litigation, etc. | Trials (Rape)—Wisconsin. | Trials (Murder)—Wisconsin. | Murder investigation—Wisconsin. | Rape investigation—Wisconsin. | Evidence, Criminal—Wisconsin. | Eyewitness identification—Wisconsin. | Judicial error—Wisconsin. | BISAC: TRUE CRIME / Murder / General. | LAW / Criminal Procedure.
Classification: LCC KF225.A84 C53 2017 (print) | LCC KF225.A84 (ebook) | DDC 345.775/02523—dc23
LC record available at https://lccn.loc.gov/2016036579

Printed in the United States of America

For Amy Kushner, PhD, with many thanks

CONTENTS

DISCLAIMERS

First, this book has not been written, published, approved, licensed, or sponsored by any person or entity that created or produced the Netflix documentary *Making a Murderer*. This book is an independent and unauthorized exploration of the legal, evidentiary, and ethical issues in the three court cases featured in the documentary.

Second, this book is not legal advice. This book should not be used for legal research or for any purpose other than entertainment and enjoyment. The author and the publisher are not responsible for any actions taken, or decisions made, by the readers of this book. Reading this book, or even contacting the author, does not create an attorney-client relationship. If you have any legal questions or legal issues of any kind, immediately call a licensed attorney in your state.

WELCOME TO THE HELLMOUTH

"That's the thrill of living on the Hellmouth. There's a veritable cornucopia of fiends and devils and ghouls to engage."[1]

Wisconsin criminal defense lawyers sometimes refer to our state as the Hellmouth. A lot of strange, inexplicable things happen here. The upside, of course, is that we defense lawyers are rarely bored. Whenever we are fighting on behalf of our clients, there is, metaphorically, "a veritable cornucopia of fiends and devils and ghouls to engage."

For example, Wisconsin is the state where a prosecutor threatened to arrest and criminally charge our school teachers for teaching sex education—even though the sex education materials had already been approved by our state's legislature and governor.[2]

Wisconsin is the state where the police are allowed to force their way into our locked, underground parking garages without a warrant.[3]

Wisconsin is the state where a judge made up facts out of thin air to justify sending a nonviolent, autistic defendant to prison—even though the prosecutor was only asking for probation.[4]

Wisconsin is the state where we put people on the sex offender registry when they've never been convicted, *or even accused*, of a sex crime.[5]

And Wisconsin is the state where a trial judge allowed the prosecutor's own employee to serve on a defendant's jury—and then our state supreme court upheld the inevitable conviction.[6]

I could go on (and on) with tales from the dark side, but my examples might simply be dismissed as anecdotal in nature. So I'll provide a compelling piece of empirical evidence: even though Wisconsin's population and demographics are nearly identical to our neighboring state, Minnesota, we incarcerate more than twice as many people.[7]

In sum, Wisconsin loves its massive, draconian, ever-expanding, and increasingly irrational criminal justice industrial complex. Given this, I wasn't at all surprised that the events in *Making a Murderer* unfolded here, on the Hellmouth, just a two-hour drive north from where I practice criminal defense.

ONE DOCUMENTARY, TWO DEFENDANTS, AND THREE JURY TRIALS

Nearly everyone who picks up this book has already seen the Netflix documentary *Making a Murderer*.[8] For those who haven't, put this book down and go watch it immediately—and allow for a sizeable block of time; once you start watching, you likely won't want to stop. For the vast majority of readers who have already seen it, the next few paragraphs will serve as a brief recap of the three court cases featured in the documentary. (The chapters that follow will discuss the facts in much more detail.)

In 1985, Steven Avery was criminally charged for the rape and beating of Penny Beerntsen in Manitowoc, Wisconsin. Avery denied the allegations and had *sixteen* alibi witnesses who placed him far away from the crime scene.[9] The state presented no physical evidence linking Avery to the crime. Yet, despite all of this, Avery was convicted based solely on the word of Beerntsen who identified him as her attacker. He spent eighteen years in prison until he was eventually exonerated by DNA evidence that proved, beyond any doubt, that serial rapist Gregory Allen was the real perpetrator.

Soon after Avery was released from prison, he filed a multimillion-dollar lawsuit against the Manitowoc Sheriff's Department and others for their role in his wrongful conviction. But shortly before key government agents were about to be deposed in the civil suit, Avery was again arrested and charged with multiple crimes—this time for allegedly murdering Teresa Halbach and burning her corpse.

In the Halbach case, unlike the Beerntsen case, the state had actual physical evidence against Avery—evidence that, on its face and according to the media, appeared to prove Avery's guilt beyond all doubt. Readers will probably remember, for example, that Halbach's car key was found inside Avery's bedroom, his blood was found inside her car, and her remains were found incinerated right outside his bedroom window. But a closer examination of the evidence revealed several problems for the state.

For example, Halbach's car key was supposedly found in plain view on Avery's bedroom floor, yet the sheriffs did not discover it until their *sixth* search of the room, thus raising the possibility that they had planted it.[10] As for Avery's blood inside Halbach's car, there was a strong argument that the sheriffs planted that evidence from a vial of his blood they had kept from the earlier Beerntsen case. And with regard to Halbach's physical remains, there was evidence that her body was not incinerated near Avery's trailer; rather, it appears she was killed and incinerated elsewhere, and then her remains were transported *to* Avery's property.

The state's problems seemed to grow with each episode of *Making a Murderer*. For every piece of evidence that initially pointed to guilt, Avery's defense team presented conflicting evidence and also exposed law enforcement's motives, inconsistent stories, and, at the very minimum, incredibly shoddy investigative work.

In the end, however, none of it mattered. Even though seven of the jurors initially voted that Avery was not the perpetrator, they eventually compromised: the jury found Avery *not* guilty of mutilating the corpse after the murder, but *guilty* of the murder itself—an irrational verdict if ever there was one. The end result was that Avery was tried and convicted again, and this time was sentenced to life in prison.

Finally, the most bizarre of the three cases featured in *Making a Murderer* was Brendan Dassey's. Law enforcement targeted Avery's sixteen-year-old, learning-disabled nephew, Dassey, in hopes of building a stronger case against Avery for the Halbach murder. If the cops could turn Dassey into Avery's coactor, instead of his alibi, the prosecutor would have a huge advantage at trial. And after the cops interrogated Dassey multiple times without an attorney—including at least one interrogation that took place after an attorney had been appointed for him—they eventually got him to incriminate himself as a "party to" the murder.

It was unusual enough that Dassey's lawyer allowed government agents to interrogate his unsophisticated client—outside of the lawyer's presence, no less. But in what might be unprecedented in the history of criminal law, Dassey's lawyer and the lawyer's private investigator actually worked with the government, and against their own client, to obtain his confession. And even though Dassey's confession was contradicted by all of the objective, physical evidence—in fact, his tale was so obviously false that the state didn't even use it at Avery's trial—Dassey, too, was convicted of Halbach's murder at his own trial.

BENEATH THE SURFACE

Viewers of *Making a Murderer* are no doubt plagued by lingering questions. For example, why did Beerntsen identify Avery as her attacker when she had never seen him before and he was nowhere near the crime scene? Why did the jury believe her testimony instead of Avery's sixteen alibi witnesses? And why did it take eighteen years to discover the real perpetrator and prove that Avery was innocent?

With regard to the Halbach case, why wouldn't the judge allow Avery's defense team to argue that a specific third party, other than Avery, committed the crime? How could the jury convict Avery of murdering Halbach when the defense demonstrated that the government mishandled—and possibly even planted—the evidence? How did the interrogators get Dassey to confess to being involved when there wasn't a single piece of evidence against him? And how could the jury convict Dassey when the details of his so-called confession were unsupported, and even contradicted, by the physical evidence?

The answers to these and similar questions are not as obvious as they first seem. Instead, to get meaningful answers we will have to dig deeper into the evidence. And we will have to dig deeper into Wisconsin's criminal laws and procedures—the complex machinery that was constantly running, just beneath the surface and out of plain sight, in *Making a Murderer*.

Each of the first thirteen chapters of this book will discuss a law, procedure, rule, or category of evidence that played a significant role in Avery's or Dassey's conviction. Many of these topics, such as erroneous eyewitness identifications, false confessions, and the anemic ethics rules governing prosecutors, are problems not just in Wisconsin but nationwide. Other topics, however, are unique to Wisconsin, and include our state's truth-suppressing trial rules, our constitutionally defective burden of proof for criminal cases, and our conviction-affirming appellate court standards.

Chapter 14 recommends some badly needed legal reforms, and discusses the political nature of such reform. Chapter 15 then offers a different lens through which *Making a Murderer*, and our criminal justice system, should be viewed. Finally, the postscript updates readers on the status of Avery's and Dassey's cases.

A FEW WORDS ON SOURCES

The above recap was just a thumbnail sketch of the three criminal trials featured in *Making a Murderer*. Additional facts will be presented in each chapter, as needed. When facts from the documentary are discussed, their source—the documentary itself—will be obvious; therefore, individual citations are generally not used in these circumstances, except for direct quotations. However, all other sources—including trial court documents, appellate briefs, appellate court decisions, and secondary sources such as law review articles—will be cited in endnote form using a simplified law review (*Bluebook*) format.[11] Additionally, some endnotes will be used to discuss matters that are related, but tangential, to the topics in the main text.

So without further delay, let's dive into the details and discover how the state of Wisconsin was able to make murderers out of Avery and Dassey. And once again, welcome to the Hellmouth.

Chapter 1

EYEWITNESS (MIS)IDENTIFICATION

"I remember his face very clearly. It's like a photograph in my memory."

—Penny Beerntsen

About two decades before the Teresa Halbach murder, Steven Avery was accused of brutally attacking a woman named Penny Beerntsen. The truth, however, was that Avery never touched her. Actually, he had never even met her. In fact, the first time he ever saw her was inside the Manitowoc County Courthouse, well after the state had criminally charged him for the assault.

EYEWITNESS IDENTIFICATION TESTIMONY

Eyewitness identification testimony was the centerpiece of Avery's first trial in *Making a Murderer*. Beerntsen testified that Avery attacked her, and the jury convicted him on all counts—even though he denied committing the crime, the state had no physical evidence linking him to the crime, and sixteen alibi witnesses testified that he was nowhere near the scene of the crime.[1]

Eighteen years later, however, we learned that victim-eyewitness Beerntsen was mistaken. And we learned that the jury was wrong. Thanks to advances in DNA testing, Avery's defense team was eventually able to prove that serial rapist Gregory Allen, not Avery, was the guilty party.

Avery's first jury trial—a complete failure of the criminal justice system if ever there was one—perfectly illustrates the two problems with eyewitness identification testimony like Beerntsen's: first, such evidence is highly *unreliable*; and second, despite its unreliability, such evidence is highly *persuasive*.[2]

These two flaws have long been conspiring to convict innocent defendants. Even the Supreme Court of Wisconsin recently acknowledged that "eyewitness testimony is often hopelessly unreliable," and, worse yet, erroneous in-court identifications "are the single greatest cause of wrongful convictions *in the United States*, and are responsible for more wrongful convictions than all other causes combined."[3]

But why did Beerntsen testify that it was Avery who attacked her? And why was her testimony so persuasive to the jury? To answer these questions we need to travel back in time to the day Beerntsen was assaulted. On that day the Manitowoc Sheriff's Department set off a chain of events that, ultimately, caused Beerntsen to misidentify Avery at trial.

THE SHOW-UP IDENTIFICATION PROCEDURE

Making a Murderer presented evidence that, within hours after Beerntsen reported being attacked, the Manitowoc Sheriff's Department conducted what is known as a "show-up" procedure using a drawing of Steven Avery. In a show-up, unlike a lineup or photo array, the cops present a single suspect (or a photograph or drawing of that single suspect) to the victim, and then ask her to confirm that the suspect is, in fact, the perpetrator.[4]

On the day Beerntsen was attacked, the Manitowoc Sheriff's Department was already familiar with Avery from his previous arrests. They were also investigating him for a recent road rage incident involving a deputy's wife. Given this, they immediately targeted him as their prime (and sole) suspect in the Beerntsen case. It was even alleged that, after hearing Beerntsen describe her attacker, Deputy Judy Dvorak proclaimed, "That sounds like Steven Avery."[5]

In hindsight, of course, we know that the sheriff's department's laser-like focus on Avery was misplaced. But even back then there were major differences between Beerntsen's description of the attacker and Avery. For example, Beerntsen was adamant that she got a good, close look at her assailant and his eyes were brown. Avery's eyes, however, were bright blue.[6] Yet despite this and other discrepancies, the sheriffs were convinced that Avery was "the guy," so they retrieved his booking photo from a previous arrest. They then had a sketch artist, Deputy Gene Kusche, produce a drawing of Avery based on that booking photo.[7] Afterward, they presented the drawing to Beerntsen and asked her to confirm that Avery was, in fact, her attacker. And she complied.

This initial show-up procedure—where the sheriffs presented Beerntsen with only one suspect, Avery—is incredibly important. While eyewitness identifications are in general unreliable, show-up identifications are the most unreliable of all. In fact, show-ups are "the most grossly suggestive identification procedure now or ever used by the police."[8]

In a show-up, the crime victim naturally thinks the cops are presenting her with only one option because they *know* who committed the crime.[9] Why else would they be focusing on one particular suspect? This, in turn, makes the victim eager to positively identify the suspect presented to her. And the victim's eagerness is exacerbated if the cops explicitly tell her—as Dvorak allegedly told Beerntsen—that the victim's initial description of the attacker "sounds like" the suspect. The end result is that the victim will positively identify the suspect in the show-up, regardless of whether he is really the attacker. The suspect will then be arrested, prosecuted, and, in many cases, convicted.

The danger of the show-up procedure was well known, even decades before the Beerntsen case. In 1967, the US Supreme Court wrote that "the practice of showing suspects singly to persons for the purpose of identification, and not as part of a lineup, has been widely condemned."[10] In fact, show-ups are so suggestive, and pose such a high risk of misidentification, that even the Supreme Court of Wisconsin eventually banned their use by law enforcement—with limited exceptions.[11]

But in one of the most interesting aspects of *Making a Murderer*, the sheriffs actually denied that they conducted a show-up procedure using the drawing of Avery. Rather, they claim they first asked

Beerntsen to describe her attacker. Then, based on her description, Kusche sketched a drawing, and the drawing looked like Avery because Avery was, in fact, the perpetrator. Beerntsen then viewed the drawing and confirmed that it accurately depicted her assailant. In other words, it was Beerntsen's verbal description, with Kusche being "just the pencil," that produced the drawing.[12]

For eighteen years after Avery's conviction, this explanation seemed plausible, and even probable. But now we know that Avery did not rape Beerntsen. Therefore, when Beerntsen described her attacker, it is incredibly *unlikely* that she would have described Steven Avery—a man who was nowhere near the crime scene when she was attacked, and a man whom she had probably never even seen before.

Given what we now know, a better explanation for why the drawing precisely matched Avery's booking photo (rather than the real perpetrator) is that when Beerntsen described her attacker, the sheriffs *wanted* it to be Avery—the man they had already decided was guilty. Kusche therefore sketched a drawing based on Avery's booking photo rather than on Beerntsen's description of the attacker. The sheriffs then presented that single drawing to Beerntsen and asked her to confirm that Avery was, in fact, her assailant.[13] Thinking that the sheriffs knew what they were doing, she agreed.

In sum, *Making a Murderer* presented a persuasive case that the sheriffs *did* conduct a highly suggestive show-up procedure, and that is why Beerntsen initially misidentified Avery on the day that she was attacked. But didn't Beerntsen later identify Avery in a photo array and a lineup? And wouldn't those subsequent identification procedures cure the problem caused by the earlier, improper show-up procedure?

THE PHOTO ARRAY AND LINEUP

After the show-up, the sheriffs did conduct a more traditional photo array procedure, and then a lineup procedure, for Beerntsen's viewing. Each identification procedure forced Beerntsen to pick her attacker out from a group of people. And in each procedure, she picked Avery.

It is true that photo arrays and lineups are more reliable than show-ups. In a photo array or lineup, the victim is asked to identify the perpetrator among several—often a total of six—individuals. One of the individuals is the person that law enforcement believes is guilty of the crime, and the others will be fillers. These fillers are people who should, to some extent, resemble the suspect,[14] but are known by law enforcement to be innocent—often because they were already incarcerated on unrelated cases at the time the victim was attacked. (As Avery learned after his trial where he presented sixteen alibi witnesses, the only surefire alibi is being in jail at the time of the crime.)

Unlike show-ups, when photo arrays and lineups are properly constructed and administered, the victim will not know which person law enforcement wants her to identify. Further, the risk of misidentification is spread among the suspect and the fillers, rather than falling entirely on the suspect, as it does in a show-up.[15] Unfortunately, however, even a proper photo array or lineup cannot sanitize the witness's memory of an earlier show-up procedure—something that likely taints all subsequent identifications.

More specifically, because Beerntsen first identified Avery in the highly suggestive show-up procedure, and then identified him in the photo array and lineup, there was no way to know whether those subsequent identifications were based on her memory of him being the real perpetrator—which we now know he was not—or her memory of seeing him in the earlier show-up procedure.

Avery's appellate counsel raised this issue in his first appeal. As the appellate court put it, Avery "contends that the lineup was suggestive because he appears to have been the only person who was in both the [earlier] photo array and the lineup. . . ."[16] (It would also follow, of course, that the photo array was suggestive because Avery also appeared in the earlier show-up. This, however, was not raised on appeal; at that time, it was not even known that the sheriffs likely conducted a show-up procedure using the drawing of Avery.)

Unfortunately, the appellate court dealt with this problem simply by ignoring it, and upheld Avery's conviction without even addressing the issue of successive identifications. But since that 1987 decision, even Wisconsin's attorney general has warned that conducting multiple, successive identification procedures is dangerous and should be avoided:

An eyewitness viewing a second procedure with the same suspect may believe that the suspect's presence in both procedures suggests that authorities believe the suspect is the perpetrator. Or, an eyewitness may become confused and identify the suspect based on recognizing him/her from the prior procedure rather than from remembering the suspect's presence at the crime. In either case, the suggestiveness of the second procedure may taint the eyewitness.[17]

Taking the specific identification procedures in reverse order, then, Beerntsen's identification of Avery in the lineup was based on her memory of him from the photo array. And Beerntsen's identification of Avery in the photo array was based on her memory of him from the show-up. And we now know that Beerntsen identified him in the show-up *not* because he was the real perpetrator, but because she believed the sheriffs when they implied (or possibly even explicitly told her) that the person in the show-up, Avery, was "the guy."

In chronological order, her misidentification of Avery in the show-up led to her misidentification in the photo array, which in turn led to her misidentification in the lineup. At this point, it was all over but the shouting.

IT'S SHOWTIME!

Ultimately, Beerntsen had to identify Avery in court, at trial, for the jury. In some ways, a witness's in-court identification of a defendant is the ultimate in highly suggestive identification procedures. First, the victim-eyewitness will reasonably assume that the defendant will be present in the courtroom at the time of the trial. Second, the victim-eyewitness will also assume—again, quite reasonably—that the defendant will not be seated on the judge's bench, in the jury box, or at the prosecutor's table. This usually leaves only two people at the defense table, and the person wearing the suit and doing the talking will obviously be the defense lawyer. This, in turn, leaves only one person—the defendant—for the witness to identify as the perpetrator.

But even aside from the suggestive nature of the courtroom setup, Beerntsen's positive, in-court identification of Avery was easy to predict. After seeing him in the three out-of-court identification procedures, pointing the finger at him in court, during the trial, was a foregone conclusion. That is, the cumulative impact of those prior, out-of-court identifications "made it all but inevitable that the witness would identify the defendant [in court] whether or not he was in fact the man" who attacked her.[18]

The only question left was whether the jury would believe Beerntsen's identification or Avery's sixteen alibi witnesses. They chose Beerntsen's identification. And this demonstrates the ultimate problem with eyewitness identification testimony in court: "[T]here is almost nothing more convincing than a live human being who takes the stand, points a finger at the defendant, and says, 'That's the one!'"[19] And this is not just speculation. It has even been demonstrated in controlled studies:

> This phenomenon is best illustrated by a classic psychological study, in which three sets of mock jurors were presented with identical evidence in a mock trial. The only difference was that each set of jurors was presented with different eyewitness evidence. One group was told that no eyewitness existed, and only 18% voted to convict. Another group heard a store clerk testify that he saw the defendant commit the crime, and 72% voted to convict, despite the defense lawyer's argument that the clerk was mistaken. Amazingly, when the third group learned that the store clerk "was legally blind and not wearing his glasses at the time" of the crime, an incredible 68% of the jurors still voted to convict. This demonstrates how willing jurors are to simply accept eyewitness testimony without any critical evaluation whatsoever.[20]

To make matters worse, in Avery's trial the jury's willingness to accept Beerntsen's testimony was exacerbated by two things: first, Beerntsen testified she was "absolutely positive" that Avery was the perpetrator; and second, to support this claim, she insisted that "she had ample opportunity to view" her attacker at the time of the assault.[21] These two things, of course, made her identification of Avery even more *convincing*. However, these two things did not make her identification more *reliable*.

Although counter-intuitive, controlled studies demonstrate that a witness's level of confidence in identification is not correlated with the accuracy of that identification.[22] In other words, a confident witness can be mistaken just as a cautious or tentative witness can be mistaken. As we know from our experience in everyday life, just because someone is more confident in remembering things doesn't mean that person's self-confidence is justified. Beerntsen simply failed to realize that her memory was a false one, and had been contaminated by the Manitowoc Sheriff's Department's multiple, pretrial identification procedures.

And perhaps even more surprising, an eyewitness's "opportunity to view" the perpetrator at the time of the crime "does not translate into an eyewitness being able to accurately recall the suspect."[23] There are at least two reasons for this: first, in hindsight, the witness can easily misstate her degree of attention during the crime; and second, the witness often fails to appreciate the impact that stress and anxiety have on her ability to focus during the crime and, later, to accurately recall the perpetrator in court.[24]

In sum, Beerntsen's in-court identification of Steven Avery—though confident and convincing—was no more accurate than the highly suggestive show-up procedure on which it, and the state's entire case, was based.

DOUBLE THE DAMAGE

Misidentifications and wrongful convictions are a huge problem with eyewitness identification evidence—particularly when those identifications are the result of, or have been tainted by, a show-up procedure. But this is really only half of the story.

It is important to remember that whenever a witness misidentifies a suspect, that suspect will be arrested, prosecuted, and possibly convicted—all while the real perpetrator remains free to commit more crimes.[25] This point can be lost on the police, prosecutors, and judges who are often determined to convict someone—*anyone*—whenever a crime is committed.

As discussed earlier, the Supreme Court of Wisconsin eventually banned the use of show-up procedures in most circumstances, including situations where the cops plan to take the suspect into custody.[26] The court reasoned that if the police are going to arrest the suspect, then he isn't going anywhere anytime soon, thus giving the police ample time to assemble a more reliable photo array or lineup for the victim's viewing. This, in turn, will reduce the risk that the victim will misidentify an innocent suspect.

Yet, despite the reasonableness of this rule, government agents still look for disingenuous ways to circumvent it. In several cases, Wisconsin prosecutors and trial judges have conspired to produce this line of reasoning: despite the ban on show-ups in situations where the police are going to arrest the suspect, a show-up procedure should still be permitted when the police plan to arrest the suspect for something *other than* the crime under investigation, such as a probation hold or arrest warrant in an unrelated case.

Fortunately, the appellate court eventually rejected this frivolous distinction and held that the reason for the suspect's arrest is irrelevant.[27] Instead, the point is that whenever the suspect is in custody, *regardless of the reason*, the police will have ample time to administer a more reliable identification procedure. Therefore, under such circumstances, the police have no justification for using a highly suggestive and error-prone show-up procedure.

For the short-sighted Wisconsin police, prosecutors, and judges who continue to look for ways around the general ban on show-ups, they should simply think of the Beerntsen case. They should remember that, when Beerntsen misidentified Avery in the show-up procedure, not only was an innocent man arrested, prosecuted, convicted, and imprisoned, but the real perpetrator—serial rapist Gregory Allen—remained free to commit more sex crimes and victimize more women before he was eventually caught. The lesson: show-up identification procedures double the damage and should rarely, if ever, be permitted in our criminal justice system.

ALIBIS VERSUS EYEWITNESSES

When the police assemble lineups and photo arrays, they need to locate five other people—known as fillers—to include along with the suspect. If the victim identifies one of the fillers as the perpetrator, the filler is not at any risk of being prosecuted. Instead, the police will know that the victim's identification was mistaken, as the filler has an airtight alibi: he was in jail on an unrelated matter at the time of the crime.

But is being in custody the *only* airtight alibi? Avery learned that his sixteen-witness alibi defense was far from airtight; the prosecutor easily defeated it with a single eyewitness. But in perhaps the most ironic eyewitness identification case of all time, a man named Donald Thomson learned that, sometimes, alibi defenses do work.

In 1975, a woman had been watching television when a man broke into her home, attacked and raped her, and left her unconscious. When she woke up she contacted the police and described Thomson as her attacker; the police were able to arrest him the next day. Fortunately for Thomson, he, just like the fillers described above, had an airtight alibi. But Thomson was not in jail at the time of the crime. Rather, he was far away from the crime scene and was being interviewed on a live television show. It turns out that the woman had been watching that same television show immediately before she was attacked, and confused Thomson's face (that she had seen on television) with the face of her assailant.[28]

That misidentification is, in one respect, similar to the Beerntsen-Avery misidentification; that is, it demonstrates how stress at the time of the event can impact the victim's future ability to accurately identify the suspect. But the irony is that Donald Thomson was a research psychologist and was invited on the television show to discuss the flaws in human memory and eyewitness identifications.[29]

It's a good thing that Thomson's television show was live, rather than tape-delayed, or his airtight alibi would have vanished. Without it, he may have ended up, like Avery, a convicted criminal instead of an ironic (and iconic) example of the hopeless unreliability of eyewitness testimony.

Chapter 2

NEWLY DISCOVERED EVIDENCE

"[T]his system is designed to perpetuate a conviction as opposed to examine whether . . . someone could in fact be innocent. . . ."

—Steve Glynn

W hen I first opened my criminal defense practice in January 2002, I started with the naïve belief that trial judges would be wary of wrongfully convicting an innocent defendant, and would therefore err on the side of caution in all judicial decision making. And even if something at the trial-court level went wrong, there would still be nothing to fear. Defendants have the right to appeal their convictions, and the appellate court would be waiting, chomping at the bit to stamp out any errors that happened to slip through. At least that's how I thought the system worked.

But after a few months of practicing law, I completely abandoned my unfounded beliefs and stood corrected.

TRIED AND CONVICTED

It is undisputed that innocent people are convicted of crimes they did not commit. In many cases, these wrongful convictions come to light through DNA exonerations. However, the overwhelming majority of real-life criminal cases do not involve DNA evidence, or even scientific evidence of any kind.[1] It is therefore extremely difficult to estimate the number of wrongful convictions that occur every year in the United States. That is why it is so important that post-conviction courts and appellate courts calmly and rationally analyze all convictions and correct any injustice—or, again, at least that's the idea.

An excellent example of the post-conviction and appeals process gone wrong is Steven Avery's conviction in the Penny Beerntsen case. The eyewitness identification aspect of that case was the subject of the previous chapter. To briefly recap the trial evidence, Beerntsen testified that she was positive Avery was her attacker. Despite her confidence, however, her initial description of the perpetrator did not match Avery in several respects. The most glaring example was that she told deputies she got a good look at the perpetrator, and he had brown eyes. Avery's booking photo, however, revealed that his eyes were bright blue.[2]

In addition to the discrepancies between Beerntsen's description of her attacker and Avery himself, Avery denied committing the crime, sixteen alibi witnesses testified that he was nowhere near the crime scene, and, most compelling of all, the state had no physical evidence linking him to the crime. Yet, despite this gross imbalance in the evidence, the jury went the other way: it found Avery guilty beyond a reasonable doubt of the false imprisonment, sexual assault, and attempted murder of Beerntsen.[3] What followed Avery's trial-court conviction was a long, winding road of judicial ineptitude.

AVERY'S FIRST APPEAL

After the jury's guilty verdicts on all counts, the case proceeded with an appeal based in part on an insufficient evidence type of claim.[4] That is, Avery argued that a single witness's identification was simply not enough evidence to sustain his conviction given the facts of his case.

This, it would seem, would be the type of case at which an appellate court would want to take a close look. How could a single witness's in-court identification of a defendant sustain a conviction given the overwhelming evidence that the defendant was innocent?

In reality, though, appellate courts do not want to do anything to disturb a jury's guilty verdict. And in this case, the court was able to easily dispense with Avery's appeal, dismissing his argument as "unmeritorious based on well-established Wisconsin law indicating that the eyewitness testimony of a victim is sufficient to sustain a conviction *even absent corroborating evidence.*"[5]

Worse yet, despite the discrepancies between Beerntsen's initial description of her attacker and Avery's appearance, the court still concluded that "her initial description *substantially matched* Avery's appearance. . . ."[6] In a subsequent appeal—an appeal discussed later in this chapter—the court at least acknowledged the eye color discrepancy. However, the court quickly dismissed the problem: "She stated that although she had initially told the police that her assailant had brown eyes, she realized when she identified him in a photograph that she was 'mistaken.'"[7]

But doesn't this "mistake" call into question the entire eyewitness identification on which the conviction was based? If Beerntsen was "mistaken" about what her attacker looked like, then how could the appellate court rely on her identification of Avery as the sole basis for the conviction? And if Beerntsen was *not* "mistaken"—that is, if her initial description was correct and she merely changed that description to conform to the physical characteristics of the suspect the sheriffs selected for her—wouldn't that, too, cast serious doubt on her identification of Avery as the perpetrator? In fact, wouldn't that be proof that Avery was innocent?

Apparently not, as the appellate court was comfortable affirming Avery's conviction. And normally, defendants don't get more than one kick at the cat during the appeals process. But in the decade following Avery's first appeal, new evidence started to trickle in, and his case for a new trial became even more compelling.

AVERY'S POST-CONVICTION MOTIONS

As time passed and DNA testing became more sophisticated, Avery's defense team asked the trial court for additional testing of the DNA evidence in his case. His post-conviction motion stated, "DNA testing which excludes both the victim and Mr. Avery would be highly significant new evidence indicating that the one-witness identification was inaccurate and that Mr. Avery's 16 alibi witnesses were correct."[8]

Perhaps thinking that Avery would merely be sending his appellate lawyer on a wild goose chase, the trial court agreed, and "granted Avery's motion for release and testing of the evidence."[9] But then the evidence came back with results that the state and the trial court did not like: "DNA analysis of the fingernail scrapings from the victim . . . reveal the presence of DNA which could not have come from either the victim or Mr. Avery and . . . most likely came from the perpetrator of this offense."[10]

In other words, because the victim engaged in a violent struggle with her attacker, the medical personnel wisely obtained samples of the material lodged under her fingernails. And now, DNA testing revealed that the biological material in those samples came from a person other than the victim and Steven Avery. Based on this and other newly discovered evidence—the state had previously failed to disclose that another suspect (the actual perpetrator, Gregory Allen) was being investigated for the crime—Avery asked for a new trial.

The trial judge, however, denied Avery's motion. Even though the judge previously agreed that "DNA testing which excludes both the victim and Mr. Avery would be highly significant new evidence," he apparently changed his mind when he said, "I conclude that the DNA evidence does not raise a reasonable probability of a different result as I view the evidence on both sides nor does it cause the Court to have doubt about the integrity of the first trial."[11]

Fortunately for Avery, he had the right to appeal the trial judge's ruling. Surely the appellate court would not fail him a second time.

AVERY'S SECOND APPEAL

We now come to the court opinion that Steve Glynn, one of Avery's civil rights lawyers, was referring to when he said that the system is "designed to perpetuate a conviction as opposed to examine whether . . . someone could in fact be innocent. . . ."[12] In Avery's second appeal, the court addressed two issues: the legal standard for review and, when applying this legal standard, whether Avery should get a new trial so he could present his newly discovered DNA evidence and third-party guilt evidence to a jury.

Avery argued that the proper legal standard was simply for the court to decide whether it was "*reasonably probable* that a different result would be reached on a new trial"—a trial where the jury would have the benefit of hearing his new evidence.[13] But the court made Avery's burden tougher to satisfy by deciding that the proper legal standard "requires the defendant to prove, *by clear and convincing evidence*, that it is *reasonably probable* that a different result would be reached on a new trial."[14]

The court had added a second burden of proof—"clear and convincing evidence"—which is a higher burden than "reasonably probable." Such legal gymnastics were intended to allow the court to conclude, with a straight face, that Avery's newly discovered DNA evidence would not change the outcome of the case if presented to a new jury in a new trial. The court's double-burden linguistic trick is the equivalent of telling a corporate plaintiff in a breach of contract case that not only do you have to prove your case by the preponderance of the evidence, but you have to prove beyond a reasonable doubt that you proved your case by the preponderance of the evidence.

If this sounds like disingenuous nonsense, it is. A few years later in an unrelated case, the Supreme Court of Wisconsin held that combining the two burdens of proof—deciding whether there is "clear and convincing evidence" of a "reasonable probability" of something happening—is irrational. The court stated that "there need only be a reasonable probability that a different result would be reached in a trial. There are no gradations of a reasonable probability; either there is one, or there is not."[15]

But even before Wisconsin's high court weighed in on this issue, it is not clear why the lower appellate court engaged in such irrational word play just to create a new hurdle for Avery. This appellate court was going to deny Avery's appeal on substantive grounds anyway, so the linguistic tricks weren't even worth its trouble. That is, the appellate court agreed with the trial judge and found Avery's newly discovered evidence to be unpersuasive—and it would have done so regardless of the legal standard it pretended to apply.

Before we discuss the appellate court's substantive decision, let's briefly recap what it knew when it rendered its decision. It knew that the state had produced one piece of evidence at trial: the eyewitness identification by Penny Beerntsen. However, that in-court identification was impeached with her prior, inconsistent description of the perpetrator and, further, was tainted by multiple, flawed, pretrial identification procedures. On the other hand, Avery had sixteen alibi witnesses and the complete lack of physical evidence on his side. And now, his newly discovered evidence included proof that law enforcement had suspected a third party for the Beerntsen rape, and proof that the DNA evidence under the victim's fingernails did not belong to either Avery or the victim. With all of this, one would expect that the appellate court would be eager to remand the case for a new trial.

That, however, was not what happened. Instead, despite all of the evidence on Avery's side of the ledger, the appellate court held that "we do not view this case as extremely close."[16] Therefore, the court concluded, Avery's newly discovered evidence "did not create a reasonable probability of a different result on retrial."[17] The court simply declared that Avery's third-party suspect evidence was "far too vague,"[18] and dismissed his new DNA evidence in the following manner:

> [T]he State argues that a source of DNA, such as a "flake" of skin, could have been deposited under [Beerntsen's] fingernails during any one of her "casual contacts" with . . . the man and woman who assisted her, her husband and hospital personnel. . . . As such, the State contends that "the DNA testing which excluded the defendant and the victim as the source of the DNA, really does not have much probative force in excluding the defendant as the assailant."
>
> *We agree with the State.* . . . [T]his evidence if used at trial would invite a fact finder to speculate about various possible sources of the DNA. In short, *the DNA evidence does not make it any more or less probable that Avery assaulted [Beerntsen].*[19]

In its desperation to deny Avery a new trial and affirm his conviction, this appellate court did not sufficiently consider—or simply did not care—how absurd its opinion would sound in any other context.

Imagine, for a moment, that a victim was beaten and assaulted, just as Beerntsen had been, during a violent struggle with her attacker. And further imagine that, in our hypothetical example, the victim knew her attacker: it was one of her roommates. In a situation like this, law enforcement would obtain DNA scrapings from under the victim's fingernails. This, of course, would provide physical evidence to corroborate the victim's accusation against her roommate-attacker.

Yet, according to the reasoning employed by Avery's appellate court, the police in our hypothetical example should not bother collecting the DNA scrapings, as such evidence would be meaningless. Why? Because DNA is easily deposited underneath fingernails—it could get there from a mere "flake of skin" that originated from "casual contacts" between the victim and the roommate-attacker *before* the attack. Therefore, even *if* the roommate's DNA was found lodged under the victim's fingernails, it would "not make it any more or less probable" that the roommate was, in fact, the attacker.

This pseudo-reasoning is a prime example of a court first deciding the conclusion it wishes to reach—in Avery's case, denying his request for a new trial—and then saying anything, no matter how absurd, to justify its predetermined outcome.

ALL'S WELL THAT ENDS WELL?

Fortunately for Avery, he was eventually cleared of the Beerntsen rape and released from prison—albeit nearly two decades after he was convicted at trial.

However, Avery's freedom was won without any help whatsoever from the conviction-affirming appellate court. Instead, additional advances in DNA technology allowed the defense to test a hair that had been collected from Beerntsen's person immediately after the rape. This test proved that the hair was not Avery's and was not the victim's. Further, the test proved that the hair belonged to Gregory Allen, a serial rapist who was serving a prison sentence for a rape he committed after raping Beerntsen. With this conclusive proof of Avery's innocence, even the prosecutor had to join in his request for freedom.[20]

Justice, however, was not only delayed, but also temporary. Unfortunately for Avery, it wasn't long before the Manitowoc Sheriff's Department arrested him again—this time for the murder of Teresa Halbach.

Chapter 3

SEEK, AND (EVENTUALLY) YE SHALL FIND

"At one point we found a key. . . . It was on the floor when we found it."

—Deputy Daniel Kucharski

"And the first time [the slippers] were moved, nobody saw the key?"

—Avery's preliminary hearing counsel

"The key wasn't there the first time they were moved."

—Deputy Daniel Kucharski

About two years after Steven Avery was released from prison, a young photographer named Teresa Halbach was reported missing. And just as they had done twenty years earlier in the Penny Beerntsen case, the Manitowoc Sheriff's Department made Avery their sole suspect. But this time, unlike the earlier Beerntsen investigation, the sheriffs eventually produced some actual physical evidence. This evidence, the state claimed, proved that Avery kidnapped Halbach, murdered her, and incinerated her body just a stone's throw from his bedroom window.

At the time Halbach went missing, Avery was suing the Manitowoc Sheriff's Department for millions of dollars for his previous, wrongful conviction. And because of the sheriff's obvious conflict of interest, the Halbach investigation was being conducted by other law enforcement agencies. No one from the Manitowoc Sheriff's Department was supposed to be involved in the investigation, let alone actively searching Avery's property. Yet, it was the Manitowoc sheriff deputies who claim to have found the physical evidence that linked Avery to the crime.

Given these highly unusual and suspicious circumstances, wouldn't Avery be able to invoke his constitutional right of privacy to protect him from another wrongful conviction?

THE FOURTH AMENDMENT

The Fourth Amendment to the United States Constitution protects "[t]he right of the people to be secure in their persons, houses, papers, and effects. . . ."[1] Further, the US Supreme Court held that the "physical entry of *the home* is the chief evil against which the wording of the Fourth Amendment is directed."[2]

In *Making a Murderer*, the officers from the Manitowoc Sheriff's Department entered Avery's home and searched it. In fact, they did so multiple times. On their *sixth* entry and search, they allegedly found the key to Teresa Halbach's vehicle—the key they claimed was sitting on his bedroom floor in plain sight, yet somehow was overlooked during their first five searches. The key was a critical piece of evidence for the state, as it helped link Avery to Halbach.

The documentary made a compelling case that the key had not been overlooked during the earlier searches; rather, it may have been planted there on the sixth search by the Manitowoc Sheriff's Department—the agency that was supposedly barred from any meaningful participation in the investigation. The defense argument, essentially, was this: had the key really been sitting on the floor, it would have been discovered during one of the first five searches where officers were literally on their hands and knees for hours, combing the room for even the smallest pieces of evidence.

This trial defense may sound persuasive but, as defense attorney Dean Strang said, blaming the cops for planting evidence is the defense lawyer's last resort, not his first choice—particularly in a government-loving community like Manitowoc, Wisconsin. Therefore, before trial, the defense team asked the judge to suppress, or exclude, the key so that the jury would never see it or hear about it.[3] One of their arguments was that law enforcement violated Avery's Fourth Amendment rights by entering and searching his home a sixth time.

The judge denied the motion, the state used the key at trial, and, as Strang had feared, the jury ultimately believed the government—or at least believed that the government was framing a guilty man. After Avery was convicted, he appealed the trial judge's ruling and argued, again, that law enforcement violated his Fourth Amendment rights.[4] Therefore, Avery claimed, he should get a new trial where the state would have to prove his guilt without using this (literally and figuratively) key piece of evidence.

THE NATURE OF THE FOURTH AMENDMENT

Despite the Supreme Court's lofty language about the noble purpose of the Fourth Amendment and the sanctity of the home, judges do not like the constitutional right of privacy. And they are not alone in this view. Most people outside of the legal profession view the Fourth Amendment as a mere "technicality" that protects only the guilty.

To illustrate this, a comparison to another constitutional right, the Sixth Amendment right of confrontation, will be helpful. Assume that a defendant is charged with burglarizing a victim's home. At trial, the state calls a witness who claims to have seen the defendant commit the crime. In such a case, the defendant has the Sixth Amendment right "to be confronted with the witnesses against him," which, for our purposes, means the defendant's lawyer is allowed to cross-examine the witness.[5] The topics for cross-examination might include the witness's ability to see the events in question, the witness's ability to accurately remember what he now claims to have seen, and, perhaps most significantly, the witness's bias, motive, and prejudice against the defendant.

In this burglary example, if the trial judge were to prevent the defense lawyer from cross-examining the witness and the defendant was convicted, the appellate court would probably agree that the defendant's Sixth Amendment right of confrontation was violated.[6] The reason: if the defense lawyer is not permitted to test the credibility of the accuser through cross-examination, then we have no way of knowing whether the defendant is actually guilty.

The Fourth Amendment right of privacy, however, is very different from the Sixth Amendment right of confrontation. In a Fourth Amendment challenge, it is the rare case that a defendant says the physical evidence he is trying to suppress was planted. (And even in those rare cases, few people will believe him.) Rather, when a defendant moves to suppress evidence, his guilt has already been established. Therefore, if a judge were to grant the defendant's motion and suppress the evidence, a guilty person will evade the government's reach, thereby escaping his (presumably) just punishment.[7]

This makes the Fourth Amendment very unpopular with judges. To paraphrase prosecutor Ken Kratz's closing argument in Avery's trial, the popular view is that constitutional rights are only for the innocent—or at least those who might be innocent. The Fourth Amendment, on the other hand, only benefits the guilty. In fact, if the defendant was innocent, there would be no evidence to suppress, and there would be no Fourth Amendment issue to begin with.

This is the unfortunate, anti-privacy backdrop against which Avery's Fourth Amendment challenge—and the Fourth Amendment challenges of defendants across the country—must be viewed.

THE REASONABLENESS CLAUSE

When the police obtain a warrant to search a suspect's home, the suspect-turned-defendant can later challenge that search by arguing that the warrant was improperly issued by the judge. An egregious example of improperly issued warrants is the Georgia judge who was caught pre-signing a stack of warrants for law enforcement officers to use as they saw fit.[8] Such disdain for our privacy rights, quite obviously, defeats the purpose of the Fourth Amendment's warrant requirement: to ensure independent review by a (hopefully) neutral and detached magistrate.

Avery's appellate lawyers, however, did not challenge the court's issuance of the warrant. Rather, they challenged the way that law enforcement carried out, or "executed," the warrant. In so doing, they relied on "the reasonableness clause" of the Fourth Amendment, which "requires that warrants be *reasonably* executed" by the government agents who search the defendant's home.[9]

Perhaps the most dreaded word for any criminal defense lawyer is the word "reasonable," along with all of its variations such as "reasonably" and "reasonableness." When the defense lawyer sees this word as part of a legal test or standard, he knows his client's ship is sunk. The word reasonable is so vague and flexible that, when placed in even the most inept judicial hands, any law enforcement action can be justified after the fact. But fortunately for Avery's appellate lawyers, in the Fourth Amendment context there are two surprisingly specific sub-rules that define what is reasonable. These sub-rules, in turn, should constrain judicial abuse of our privacy rights—at least in theory.

First, in order to be reasonable, "searches are subject to the 'one warrant, one search' rule."[10] And for good reason, because if the police could get a warrant and then search and search again, as often as they wished, the "warrant could become a means of tyrannical oppression in the hands of an unscrupulous officer to the disturbance or destruction of the peaceful enjoyment of the home. . . ."[11] Therefore, when the police get a warrant to search a suspect's home, the reasonableness clause demands that they conduct their search, and then get out and stay out.

And there is a second sub-rule to help define what is reasonable: when searching, the police may only seize items authorized by the warrant.[12] For example, a very common search warrant in Wisconsin is one that permits the police to enter and search a person's home for drug evidence—typically marijuana. (Citizens of Colorado and some other states probably cannot imagine such a search occurring at all, let alone with regularity.) When executing such a warrant, the police would probably violate the reasonableness clause if, during their search, they also seized the defendant's collection of philosophy books. (Surprisingly, however, taking the defendant's phone, computer, money, and personal documents might very well be permitted depending on the language of the warrant—but that is a matter for another book.)

Given these two specific sub-rules designed to constrain judicial abuse when deciding, after the fact, whether a search was reasonable, Avery's appellate lawyers appeared to be on solid ground. In fact, we don't even have to go beyond the first sub-rule. The judge's legal analysis, for Avery's case, should have gone as follows. Issue: did law enforcement officers violate the Fourth Amendment when they searched Avery's trailer a sixth time and allegedly found Halbach's car key? Rule: "One warrant, one search." Analysis: six is more than one. Conclusion: suppress the evidence.

But such an analysis would be too simple, too clear, and would not serve the government's interests. Therefore, the courts have created an exception to the sub-rule.

THE RETURN OF "REASONABLE"

Unfortunately for Avery, "courts have recognized an *exception* to the 'one warrant, one search' rule where a subsequent entry and search are a *reasonable continuation* of the earlier one."[13] These reasonable continuation searches are permitted, and any evidence obtained in those searches can be used against the defendant at trial.

There is that word "reasonable" again, and it nearly always spells doom for the defendant. Recall that we began with the rule that police must execute a search warrant reasonably. Then we got a much-needed sub-rule that offered specificity and structure: "one warrant, one search." But now the courts have developed an exception to the sub-rule that returns us to the much vaguer and more flexible reasonableness standard. In a sense, we've come full circle.

The question, then, under this exception, is whether law enforcement's sixth search of Avery's home was a reasonable continuation of the first search. To answer this question we need to dive into the facts (all of which were set forth in Avery's appellate brief and include citations to the original court transcripts).[14]

The court issued the warrant to search Avery's trailer on November 5. On this day, law enforcement conducted a quick search and left, and then went back to search more thoroughly. This second search was conducted by four officers who spent more than two hours combing through every inch of Avery's tiny 700-square-foot trailer. This search included Avery's bookcase, as well as the area between the bookcase and the bed. During this search they seized fifty items. They took everything they thought might have evidentiary value, and they believed they had completed their search. In the days that followed, law enforcement reentered Avery's trailer for various reasons a third, fourth, and fifth time. None of these first five searches produced any evidence that belonged to Halbach or that placed her in the trailer. Nor did they produce any evidence linking Avery to the crime.

On November 8, however, law enforcement officers went back into Avery's bedroom a *sixth* time and claimed to have found Halbach's car key on the floor in plain view. However, in order to make a jury believe that they didn't plant the key, they needed to explain how they could have overlooked the key in their first five searches— one of which was so thorough that the cops were on their hands and knees, literally combing the floor for microscopic evidence. Their explanation: the key was never there during the first five searches; rather, it fell out of the bookcase when Sergeant Andrew Colborn went back into the bedroom, for the sixth time, allegedly to seize Avery's pornography collection from his bookshelf.

Avery's appellate lawyers explained it this way: "[E]ven though ostensibly in the bedroom only to retrieve pornographic material from the bookcase, Sergeant Colborn . . . tipped the bookcase to the side and twisted it away from the wall."[15] Colborn even testified, "I will be the first to admit, I wasn't any too gentle, as we were, you know, getting exasperated. I handled it rather roughly, twisting it, shaking it, pulling it."[16] Then, Avery's appellate lawyers continued, "[a]fter jostling the bookcase, Colborn was 'very surprised' to see a car key lying on the floor between the bookcase and bed."[17]

It's not clear why someone taking pornography off a bookcase would tip, twist, shake, and pull the bookcase on which the pornography lay. But again, the sheriffs needed to offer some explanation for how the key simply appeared on the floor out of thin air. The problem for the sheriffs, however, was that by generating this explanation to satisfy the jury at the upcoming jury trial, they were admitting to an illegal search. And if the search was illegal, the evidence should be suppressed, and the jury would never see or hear about the key.

More specifically, Colborn's explanation proves that the sixth search was not a "reasonable continuation" of the earlier searches, for two reasons. First, the earlier, four-officer, two-plus-hour search was completed and all the evidence they wanted to collect had been collected.[18] And a warrant only allows for one search. The police had their one search, along with four reasonable continuations of that search, for a grand total of five searches. Their search was finished. There simply was nothing to be "continued" by the sixth search, and the sixth search was therefore illegal.

And second, recall the previous sub-rule that, when searching a suspect's home, law enforcement may only seize the items named in the warrant. And in this case, Colborn said that he went back into Avery's bedroom to take pornography from the bookcase. Then, in order to take the pornography, he tipped, twisted, shook, and pulled the bookcase, thus explaining the otherwise inexplicable key that appeared on the floor out of nowhere. The problem, of course, is that pornography was not listed in the warrant as an item that could be seized during the search.[19] Nor should it have been; there is nothing illegal about adult pornography, it is incredibly common, and it in no way constitutes evidence of murder. In a nutshell, law enforcement officers went beyond the scope of the warrant, their execution of the warrant was not reasonable, and the evidence discovered as a result of the sixth search must be suppressed. The key, therefore, should never have been used at trial.

But despite this logical and seemingly inescapable conclusion, we know from watching the documentary that the key *was* used at trial. (Readers may remember Avery's defense lawyer Jerry Buting holding it during trial, suggesting that, had it actually dropped from the bookcase as the sheriffs claimed, someone would have heard it.) But why was the state allowed to use the key at trial if it was found during law enforcement's illegal search and seizure? The answer is that, despite the facts, the court simply found that law enforcement's execution of the warrant was "reasonable."[20] And the court got very creative in finding ways to justify this predetermined conclusion.

For example, in their brief, Avery's appellate lawyers cited the testimony of an officer who searched Avery's room during the earlier, four-officer, two-plus-hour search. That officer testified that the search had been completed, and they had collected everything they intended to collect, days before Colborn reentered Avery's room to seize the pornography. But this government agent's testimony did not support the court's predetermined outcome. Therefore, the court simply dismissed it as "arguably ambiguous testimony" from a "mere foot soldier."[21]

Similarly, even though Colborn testified under oath about his purpose in reentering Avery's bedroom the sixth time, the court decided to look for a different explanation. The court preferred the testimony of Colborn's supervisor who claimed that Colborn was "also there to conduct a final, thorough search of the trailer."[22] The court was not at all troubled that this account conflicted with Colborn's own testimony about why he was really there and what he was actually doing.

In sum, the appellate court handled the facts of Avery's case the same way Colborn handled the bookcase: it tipped, twisted, shook, and pulled until it got what it wanted. And just as Colborn's jostling of the bookcase magically produced a key piece of evidence against Avery, so too did the appellate court's rigorous jostling of the facts magically produce its desired result. The sixth search was a reasonable continuation of the first, second, third, fourth, and fifth searches of Avery's trailer. Therefore, the court concluded that the key was properly used at trial to convict Avery.

INEVITABLE DISCOVERY

Sensing, perhaps, that its legal analysis on reasonableness stretched credulity, the appellate court used a second exception to justify law enforcement's multiple searches of Avery's trailer. This second exception would also come in handy in the unlikely event that the Supreme Court of Wisconsin were to review the case—something it ultimately, and unsurprisingly, declined to do. The appellate court held that "the fruits of an illegal search nonetheless may be admitted if the tainted fruits *inevitably* would have been discovered by *lawful means*."[23]

This inevitable discovery doctrine says that, even when law enforcement violates the Fourth Amendment in collecting evidence, the evidence can still be used against the defendant as long as the cops would have found the evidence some other way. And there are more sub-rules to apply when deciding whether the evidence would have inevitably been discovered: first, before the illegal search—here, the November 8 entry to seize Avery's pornography—the government must have had other leads and was "actively pursuing some alternate line of investigation"; and second, there was "a reasonable probability that the evidence in question"—here, the car key—"would have been discovered" through the alternate line of investigation.[24]

To decide whether the car key would have been inevitably discovered through lawful means, we must, once again, dive into the facts. The state pointed to numerous other lines of investigation that law enforcement officers pursued, including searches of Avery's property outside of his trailer where they found physical evidence linking him to the crime. In fact, all of these lines of investigation pointed to Avery as the sole suspect. Therefore, the state argued, there was a reasonable probability that the cops would have found the key anyway.[25]

Avery's appellate lawyers, however, pointed to other facts. Law enforcement had already searched Avery's room, including the bookcase, and no key was found.[26] That part of the search was completed. Had Colborn not illegally reentered the room to take Avery's pornography—again, an item not named in the search warrant and certainly not evidence of a crime—none of the other lines of investigation would have led the cops back inside the trailer, let alone to the bookcase. And there was certainly no line of investigation that would have caused them to jostle the bookcase by tipping, twisting, shaking, and pulling it.

Therefore, the defense argued, despite these other lines of investigation, "the leads did not make it inevitable that the police would look for and find the Toyota key hidden in a bookcase in Avery's bedroom."[27] There simply was not a reasonable probability that the key would have inevitably been discovered; rather, it was only discovered because of Colborn's illegal entry and seizure of the pornography.

The court, however, was persuaded by the state. The court reasoned that law enforcement was conducting a search, outside of Avery's trailer, that produced physical evidence against Avery. It then held that "[a]rmed with evidence pointing to Avery's involvement, we are satisfied that the police would have continued the search of Avery's trailer until all areas had been inspected—including that area in between Avery's bed and bookshelf where the key to Halbach's vehicle was discovered."[28]

The court's reasoning, however, misses the point. To begin, according to the cops the key was *not* just sitting "in between Avery's bed and bookshelf"; rather, it supposedly fell there during the jostling of the bookcase.[29] But that aside, the court ignores that the cops already searched Avery's trailer from top to bottom, including the four-officer, two-plus-hour search that included a search of the bookcase and a thorough search of the floor between the bed and the bookcase. So how could the court conclude that, given the evidence the cops were allegedly finding *outside*, they would have gone back *inside* to re-search Avery's trailer a seventh or eighth time? More to the point, how would the evidence they were finding outside the trailer lead to a reasonable probability that they would go back into the trailer's bedroom to jostle the bookcase?

Of course, the word "reasonable" has, once again, sunk Avery's ship. In hindsight, any court can simply decide it was reasonably probable that the illegally obtained evidence would have inevitably been discovered some other way. This exception, too, has swallowed the rule. "The doctrine of inevitable discovery [has become] an open door through which the fruits of all defective searches may be transformed into admissible evidence. The doctrine [has] become a vehicle abrogating the right of all citizens to be free from unreasonable searches and seizures."[30]

MUCH ADO ABOUT NOTHING?

The defense team's motion to suppress evidence, when viewed against the backdrop of the judiciary's disdain for the Fourth Amendment, seems like an exercise in futility. To begin with, from the judge's standpoint there is overwhelming evidence of Avery's guilt. Then, when Avery's defense team moves to suppress that evidence, the judge has numerous sub-rules, exceptions, and reasonableness tests at his disposal—all of which are designed to reach a predetermined outcome: the denial of Avery's motion to suppress and, therefore, the admission of the evidence at trial.

But even if a judge made an honest attempt to apply these intricate, hyper-technical rules in good faith, would it matter? What if the judge had found that the police had no business going back into Avery's bedroom a sixth time to take his pornography collection? What if the judge had found that, given all of the new leads being developed *outside* of Avery's home, the police would have followed *those* leads instead of nonsensically re-searching Avery's bedroom yet again? In either of these situations, would the judge really have suppressed the key and excluded it from Avery's trial?

Probably not. The reason is that, even when all of the sub-rules, exceptions, and reasonableness tests fail, the government still has one last bullet in the chamber: the Fourth Amendment right of privacy has been separated from its remedy. What this means is that, even when the defendant can clearly establish that the police violated the Fourth Amendment, this does not mean that he has a right to have the evidence excluded from trial under the so-called exclusionary rule. The US Supreme Court explains it this way:

> The fact that a Fourth Amendment violation occurred . . . does not necessarily mean that the exclusionary rule applies. Indeed, exclusion has always been our *last resort*, not our first impulse, and our precedents establish important principles that constrain application of the exclusionary rule.
>
> First, the exclusionary rule is *not an individual right* and applies only where it results in appreciable deterrence. We have repeatedly rejected the argument that exclusion is a necessary consequence of a Fourth Amendment violation. Instead, we have focused on the efficacy of the rule in deterring Fourth Amendment violations *in the future*.
>
> In addition, *the benefits of deterrence must outweigh the costs*. We have never suggested that the exclusionary rule must apply in every circumstance in which it might provide marginal deterrence. To the extent that application of the exclusionary rule could provide some incremental deterrent, *that possible benefit must be weighed against its substantial social costs*.[31]

Now, imagine this rule in the context of the Manitowoc Sheriff's Department investigating the heinous and senseless murder of Teresa Halbach. Would the benefits of possible future deterrence—that is, deterring the police from illegally seizing a suspect's pornography collection in the future—justify the "substantial social costs" of suppressing relevant evidence—the car key—in a murder case? Of course it wouldn't.

Therefore, by separating the underlying right from its remedy, the US Supreme Court has formally incorporated the Wisconsin judiciary's dislike of the Fourth Amendment into the analysis; the guiltier the defendant appears to be and the more serious the crime with which he is charged, the more likely the judge will allow the evidence to be used at trial (despite the Fourth Amendment violation in obtaining it).

Of course, this separation of the underlying right from its remedy does two things. First, it reduces the Fourth Amendment's grand language to an empty catchphrase, and second, it actually creates a misnomer. That is, with evidence rarely being excluded because of the "substantial social costs" of doing so, the exclusionary rule, if it still exists, would more accurately be called the exclusionary exception.

But regardless of whether the court relied upon the reasonable continuation exception, the inevitable discovery exception, or the social cost exception to the poorly named exclusionary rule, the outcome was predetermined before the analysis began: the key was coming into evidence at Avery's trial.

Chapter 4

WEIRD SCIENCE

"[The DNA testing protocol], ninety-nine percent of the time, it's followed. You need that guideline. You need that standard. But when you're dealing with such sensitive, sensitive, technology you have to allow an element of common sense, and this clearly called for it."

—Prosecutor Norm Gahn

The last chapter explained how the state was able to get its physical evidence past the Fourth Amendment and into Steven Avery's trial for the murder of Teresa Halbach. But much of this evidence wouldn't have meant anything without someone to interpret it for the jury. So the state called a lot of expert witnesses with a lot of scientific degrees. These experts included chemists, evidence technicians, DNA analysts, and forensic anthropologists, among others. But were these people really testifying as scientists? Or were they merely government agents attempting to cast the illusion of scientific certainty on the state's case?

THE SCIENTIFIC METHOD

Anyone familiar with science knows that the goal of the "scientific method" is to seek the truth, rather than to seek the outcome we would *like* to be true. One educational resource puts it this way: "[T]he scientific method attempts to minimize the influence of bias or prejudice in the experimenter when testing an hypothesis or a theory."[1] And with regard to the need for consistent, rigorous testing,

49

it is important not to let so-called "common sense . . . tempt us into believing that no test is needed" or—perhaps even more harmful— that methodologies and protocols can be disregarded when conducting the tests.[2]

In criminal jury trials such as Avery's, the scientists that perform the tests and then testify in court are typically government employees. And, unfortunately, their biases and prejudices can infect their testing and their ultimate opinions. Often their goal is not to seek the truth or to follow the evidence only as far as it leads; rather, their goal is to help the state convict the defendant. And in so doing, they are often willing to discard scientific methodologies and protocols, and sometimes even skip the scientific testing altogether.

It helps when skilled defense lawyers, such as Jerry Buting and Dean Strang, cross-examine the government's experts and expose their biases and prejudices. However, even then, a serious problem remains: when the state's experts use scientific jargon for the jury, their testimony puts a shiny, scientific gloss of certainty on what is nothing more than a prosecutor's argument. And this was a glaring problem throughout Avery's trial in *Making a Murderer*.

EDTA TESTING

An important piece of evidence for the state was Avery's blood inside Halbach's car. The prosecutor argued that this proved Avery killed her, got into her car, and drove it away to hide it. While doing this, the prosecutor claimed, Avery left blood in the car from a cut on his finger. Conversely, the defense argued that, if this were true, Avery's fingerprints would have also been found in the car, but they were not. Therefore, the defense argued, it was more likely that the Manitowoc Sheriff's Department planted the evidence from a vial of Avery's blood that they had kept from the Penny Beerntsen case.[3]

When physically inspecting this vial of blood, the defense (and the government agents who were present) discovered that it appeared to have been tampered with. The seal to the evidence was broken, and there was a puncture hole the size of a needle in the top of the vial. This was strong evidence to support the defense argument that someone took Avery's blood from the vial and planted it inside Halbach's car.

So how did the blood really get there? Did it come from Avery's cut finger when he got inside the car after allegedly killing Halbach? Or did the cops take it from the old blood vial and plant it? The answer came down to four letters: EDTA.

EDTA does not appear naturally in the blood. Rather, it is a preservative that was used to keep the blood in the vial from going bad. So if the bloodstains inside Halbach's car had EDTA in them, the blood was probably planted. If they did not have EDTA in them, then the blood inside the car likely came from Avery's hand and not from the vial. Unfortunately, though, no reliable test for EDTA was in current use. Therefore, the FBI—acting with unprecedented swiftness for a government agency—resurrected an EDTA test for the state of Wisconsin to use when prosecuting Avery. Not surprisingly, the test produced a negative result for EDTA; that is, EDTA was not detected in three of the bloodstains taken from inside the car. This led the state's expert—an FBI employee—to testify that the blood came from Avery's hand and not from the vial.

But that is where the problems started. The state's expert testified that none of the six stains lifted from the car contained EDTA. However, he only tested three of the six stains. The other three were never tested—either because they were not sent to him or because he only tested half of the samples he received. Yet, when Buting cross-examined him, he was still quite comfortable concluding that the other three, untested bloodstains also did not contain EDTA, and therefore did not come from the vial.

While drawing a scientific conclusion without running a test was the most egregious violation of the scientific method, the witness's second violation was not far behind: for the three samples he did test, he drew his conclusion without knowing the test's sensitivity level.

Here, an analogy to medicine can be helpful. Suppose that when humans are infected with virus A, we produce antibodies. And further suppose that scientists have developed a test to detect those antibodies. However, the test's sensitivity level is such that a person must wait three months from the suspected time of infection, at which point the test will produce a positive result in 50 percent of those patients who are *actually* infected. If the patient waits less time, or more time, the doctor will achieve a lower, or higher, confidence level.

Given this, if a patient is tested three months after a suspected exposure to virus A, and tests positive, the doctor can conclude that the patient has the virus. However, if the test result is negative, the doctor *cannot* conclude that the patient does *not* have the virus, regardless of how much the patient would like the doctor to do so. Instead, there are at least two possibilities: (1) the person does not have virus A, or (2) the person has virus A, but has not yet produced enough antibodies to trigger a positive test result.

The same general concept applies to EDTA testing. Because the sensitivity level, or "method detection limit," for the newly created test was not known, the FBI's negative result for the three *tested* samples could mean several things, including (1) there was no EDTA in the samples tested, or (2) there was EDTA in the samples tested, but the test was not sensitive enough to detect it.

And of course, with regard to the other three *untested* samples, the only valid conclusion that a scientist could draw is that she cannot render an opinion regarding the presence of EDTA. As Avery's expert witness testified, "I'm an analytical chemist. I'm not in the business of just guessing what's in samples. We have to *test* samples to decide what's in them."[4] (The sign of a true scientist—a scientist devoted to the rigorous application of the scientific method—is the reluctance to draw conclusions beyond what is warranted by the evidence.)

But again, the state's FBI-employed scientist-witness testified that, "to a reasonable degree of scientific certainty,"[5] none of the six bloodstains collected from the car came from the vial of blood. Why would he be so willing to reach this conclusion without even testing three of the six samples? And why would he be so quick to conclude, without knowing the test's method detection limit, that the tested samples did not come from the vial of blood?

The answer is found in the state's request for testing. First, on direct examination the prosecutor had the FBI witness talk about the agency's role in protecting the public from cops who plant evidence, thus allegedly explaining the FBI's interest in Avery's case. But then, on cross-examination, the defense exposed the real reason for the FBI's involvement: to "*eliminate* the allegation that this vial was used to plant evidence."[6] Although the witness denied that this was the FBI's purpose in running the test, the government's document spoke for itself.

BONES

In order to convict Avery, the state also used an expert witness to testify about Halbach's bone fragments. These fragments were recovered from a burn pit on the Avery property. The state's theory was that Avery killed her in either his trailer or garage—the state frequently flip-flopped on where—and then incinerated her corpse in the burn pit, just a few feet away. The defense, however, argued that Halbach's body was incinerated elsewhere, and her bone fragments were transported by the killer *to* the burn pit near Avery's trailer. In support of this, the defense pointed to several facts, including that two of her bone fragments were actually located far away from the burn pit, in a quarry.

The state's scientific expert, a forensic anthropologist, testified that Halbach's body was burned where the vast majority of her bones were found, in the burn pit right outside Avery's trailer. In double-negative style, she testified, "It's highly unlikely that was not the primary burn location."[7]

The basis for her confident, scientific conclusion was this: had Halbach been incinerated elsewhere and the bones been moved *to* that location near Avery's trailer, the process of moving them would have caused them to break. And because the bones that were recovered did not show evidence of such breakage, she could only conclude that the area outside Avery's trailer was, in fact, the primary burn site.

Even to the layperson, this is a rather odd conclusion. Why? Because the bones *were* broken; they were actually bone *fragments*. But that aside, on cross-examination the defense pointed out that, even to get the bones from the burn pit to the place where the expert examined them, they had, in fact, been moved. And not only had they been moved, but they were first shoveled, sifted, and handled—and none of these activities caused the type of breakage that the expert claimed should have been caused by moving them. Therefore, it was quite possible that the body had been burned elsewhere, and then the bones were transported *to* the burn pit outside Avery's trailer.

In light of this cross-examination, the state's expert simply changed her rationale, explaining that the area outside Avery's trailer was the primary burn site not because of the condition of the bones—she quickly abandoned that theory—but because that's where most of the bones were located.

Of course, this defies even common sense—the very same common sense that prosecutors claim to rely on whenever the scientific method fails to suit their needs. Consider which is more likely: (1) someone burned the body in the quarry, transported the remains to the burn pit near Avery's trailer, and, in the process, accidentally left two small bone fragments behind at the quarry; or (2) Avery burned the body in the burn pit near his trailer, picked out only two small bone fragments, and then traveled a great distance to deposit them far away in the quarry while leaving the vast majority of the bones right outside his bedroom window.

Not surprisingly, the defense expert later answered this question. Because Halbach's bones were found in two separate locations, it is undisputed that the bone fragments had, in fact, been moved. And, when bone fragments are moved, typically the place where most of the bones are found is where the bones were moved *to*, not where they were moved from.

By the end of her cross-examination, even the state's expert had to concede that the bones could have been burned elsewhere and then transported to the burn pit. Nonetheless, the jury still heard her previous testimony that Halbach's body was burned just a few feet from Avery's trailer. Whether this pseudoscientific conclusion remained ringing in the juror's ears—and whether they remembered or even heard any of the testimony after that point—is anyone's guess.

THE MAGIC BULLET

The state had two different theories of its case against Avery. One theory was based on its multiple interrogations of Avery's sixteen-year-old, learning-disabled nephew, Brendan Dassey. Under this theory,

Avery had Halbach tied up in the bedroom of his trailer where he stabbed her and even cut her throat, creating an incredibly bloody mess, before dragging her body outside, which created an even bigger bloody mess. But the problem with this theory is that the government used multiple officers, over the course of several hours and six different searches, to comb every inch of Avery's trailer. They were even on their hands and knees, painstakingly collecting evidence that was not visible to the naked eye. But in the end, even after all of their forensic testing, there was no blood, DNA, or other evidence to suggest that Halbach had even set foot in the trailer, let alone was murdered there. In fact, the forensic evidence showed that Dassey's story of a bloody stabbing and throat slashing was a pure fabrication.

In the state's other theory, Avery shot Halbach in the garage located near his trailer. Unfortunately for the state, however, officers had combed every nook and cranny of the garage and its contents, and couldn't find a single trace of blood spatter, DNA, or anything else to indicate that Halbach was ever in the garage, let alone was killed there. They even tore up the concrete garage floor, looking for blood that, had Halbach really been shot, would have inevitably found its way into the cracks and crevices in the cement. Again, the state struck out. The only conclusion was that Halbach was not killed in the garage either.

The state was desperate to find some evidence that Teresa Halbach had been inside Avery's trailer or garage. And it eventually found its magic bullet. While there was a great deal of evidence that guns were fired regularly on the Avery property—not surprising given all of the hunting that went on there—the state claims to have found a spent bullet in Avery's garage. Hoping that it had Halbach's DNA on it, the state sent it for testing.

When testing things for DNA, there is a protocol: if the analyst obtains a positive result, but there is also evidence of contamination, the analyst must declare the test to be inconclusive rather than positive. To demonstrate, consider this common, well-documented example of laboratory contamination. A government analyst is testing evidence in the case of *State v. Jones*. He tests an object—say, a comb—and obtains a positive result for Jones's DNA. He puts the Jones case away and moves on.

Several weeks later, the analyst tests the evidence in the completely unrelated case of *State v. Smith*. He tests an object—say, a drinking glass—and obtains a positive result for Smith's DNA. But he also receives a positive result for Jones's DNA. How did Jones's DNA get on Smith's drinking glass? It obviously came from the previous test of the comb in the Jones case, but we don't know how it found its way onto the glass in the Smith case. The test therefore must be declared inconclusive due to the contamination. If there is enough of a sample remaining on the drinking glass to retest, then a retest can be done. If not, then the final answer is that the test of the glass in the Smith case is inconclusive.

And that is the precise protocol that the state's DNA analyst followed every single time—until the Avery case where she tested the state's magic bullet. In Avery's case, the test on the bullet came back positive for Teresa Halbach's DNA. However, it also came back positive with the DNA of another person: the analyst herself. The sample had been contaminated.

How did the analyst's DNA get on the bullet? She could speculate (and did), but she simply did not know. And given that her own DNA could not be explained, neither could Halbach's. Was Halbach's DNA on the bullet because she had been shot with it? (There was no visible blood on it or anywhere near it, so that conclusion was contradicted by the evidence.) Or was Halbach's DNA on the bullet because her DNA was present in the lab from previous items that were analyzed—for example, her own bloodstains found inside her own car—and then got transferred onto the bullet, similar to what happened in the Jones and Smith cases above? The ultimate question, then, is this: if the analyst's DNA was present in the room and got transferred onto the bullet, how do we know that the same thing didn't happen with Halbach's DNA?

We don't know, of course, and that's why the state's own scientific-testing protocol demands that the test be declared inconclusive, and that another sample must be taken from the bullet for retesting. Unfortunately for the state, however, the entire sample had been used up in the first test and there was nothing left. Therefore, instead of declaring the test inconclusive, the state disregarded the protocol and the analyst testified that the bullet tested positive for Halbach's DNA.

The media asked prosecutor Norm Gahn this question about the analyst's own DNA appearing on the bullet: "If it's not a big deal, and it's a good sample, then why is the rule that you should toss it?"[8]

Prosecutor Gahn responded, a bit frustrated, "Because I think the rule—well, I don't think anyone tossed it here."[9]

That's right, Norm, but that was the point of the question. We know the analyst did *not* toss it. The question was, if the sample is still good, as you are saying it is, then why does the rule say that it *should have been* tossed?

Prosecutor Gahn then continued with the quote from the very beginning of this chapter: "The rule, ninety-nine percent of the time, it's followed. You need that guideline. You need that standard. But when you're dealing with such sensitive, sensitive, technology you have to allow an element of *common sense*, and this clearly called for it."[10]

This time, he does more than merely sidestep the media's question or miss the point of the question. This time, he actually misstates the purpose of the protocol. It is *because* we have "sensitive, sensitive technology" that we need the testing protocol in the first place. The sensitivity of the technology is not an excuse to violate the protocol; rather, it is the reason *for* the protocol.

Prosecutor Gahn and the state's DNA analyst—along with the state's EDTA analyst from the FBI—fell prey to the very thing the scientific method is designed to eliminate: the temptation, based on so-called common sense, to believe that test protocols, or even the tests themselves, can be disregarded in order to arrive at the conclusion they want to reach.

The danger of disregarding science in favor of so-called common sense is obvious; the "sense" alleged to be "common" really isn't. Rather, it depends on what the so-called expert wants to accomplish.[11] Just as with the state's FBI witness who wanted to rule out the presence of EDTA in the blood samples, the DNA analyst's goal in testing the bullet was equally clear. The lead investigator had contacted her before she tested the bullet and instructed her, "Try to put [Halbach] in his house or garage."[12] When the marching orders are that clear, then it makes perfect "common sense" to disregard the protocol and declare the test positive for Halbach's DNA. And once again, bias and prejudice have worked their way into the scientific process.

A MATTER OF PERSPECTIVE

The above discussion demonstrates that, when scientific tests are skipped and protocols are ignored, determining what is common sense really depends on one's perspective. And this perspective, in a larger sense, explains why science in criminal cases is infected with human error, biases, prejudices, and motives.

For example, consider the method of transmission for DNA evidence. In Avery's first case—where he was wrongfully convicted for the rape and attempted murder of Penny Beerntsen—the defense was hopeful when, many years after the conviction, DNA testing advanced to the point where the evidence could be retested. And the defense thought they hit the jackpot when Beerntsen's fingernail scrapings tested positive for DNA that did not belong to her or Avery. Despite this, the prosecutor, trial judge, and appellate court concluded that such evidence did not justify a new trial. Their reasoning was that the DNA could have easily found its way under Beerntsen's fingernails from any number of casual contacts, including from a towel or merely from sitting with the people who found her after the attack. Therefore, the government said, the third party's DNA lodged under Halbach's fingernails was so unpersuasive that Avery was not entitled to a new trial.[13]

Now consider the reasoning in the Halbach case when the DNA analyst tested the bullet. We know that DNA is so easily transferred that the analyst's own DNA got onto the bullet during the testing process. In fact, the state's own protocol recognized this and required that the analyst declare the test inconclusive. Nonetheless, the state flip-flopped its position from the Beerntsen case. This time, the government decided, contamination was not a risk, it was okay to disregard the protocol, and common sense dictated that Halbach's DNA on the bullet proved she had been shot with the bullet—even though there was no blood on it, near it, or anywhere in the garage.

In short, the government's common sense is far from common. Rather, it has a chameleon-like quality, and tends to shift and morph depending on the needs of any given situation.

WISCONSIN'S NEW DAUBERT STANDARD

In theory, there is a legal explanation for how the state was able to pass junk science off as science in Avery's case. In Wisconsin during that time, there was an incredibly lax standard for the state's use of expert testimony. Essentially, the prosecutor could call virtually anyone as an expert, and that so-called expert could testify to virtually anything. Then, it was up to the jury to sort it out and make sense of it.[14] And this lax standard posed a significant problem: the state was always able to use a so-called expert to paint the face of credibility on a garbage case. And even when the defense was able to effectively cross-examine the state's expert, this would only be meaningful if the jury was interested in, and capable of understanding, nuanced topics such as scientific testing protocols and method detection limits. In many instances, even assuming the jurors had not prejudged the defendant, they simply didn't care about or understand the scientific concepts being debated at trial. In the end, all they really heard was the government's so-called expert concluding that the defendant was guilty.

Since Avery's trial, however, Wisconsin has moved to the nationally recognized Daubert standard for the admissibility of expert testimony.[15] This standard, in theory, is tougher to satisfy. Under Daubert, the state is not permitted to use an expert unless the testimony "is based upon sufficient facts or data" and "is the product of reliable principles and methods," and "the witness has applied the principles and methods reliably to the facts of the case."[16]

However, like many of the legal standards in criminal law, this one is factor-laden and can be twisted and turned as easily as the bookcase in Avery's bedroom (see chapter 3). When determining whether the testimony "is the product of reliable principles and methods," courts can pick and choose from among ten or more factors. "There is no definitive list of reliability factors that must be applied in all cases. Nor is there a hierarchy of factors that ranks them in order of preference or weight. Which factors apply and how they are weighed are within the court's discretion."[17]

As soon as Wisconsin announced the change to the Daubert standard for the admissibly of expert testimony, I predicted aloud, to anyone who would listen, that even under this supposedly tougher standard, courts would continue to allow the state to call any so-called expert it wished for any purpose whatsoever. And that is exactly what has happened: "In theory, Wisconsin's new test for the admissibility of expert testimony is flexible but *has teeth*. In practice, it's flexible and *has dentures*. Literally every Daubert challenge litigated on appeal since [the new law] became effective *has failed*."[18]

As a result, jury trials have been indistinguishable from those in the pre-Daubert, anything-goes era of expert testimony. In one Wisconsin case, the appellate court allowed the state to use its expert even when the "expert testimony did not neatly fit the Daubert factors."[19] The court's reason: this type of testimony was commonly ruled admissible by "pre-Daubert Wisconsin courts."[20]

That is rather curious reasoning. The legislature changed the law to take away the anything-goes standard and make it tougher to use so-called experts at trial. It would therefore seem that when the state's proposed expert testimony does "not neatly fit the Daubert factors," it should be *excluded* from evidence. And, when trying to find a way to admit such testimony under the new law, judges should probably not be allowed to rely on decisions from the "pre-Daubert Wisconsin courts," as this, too, would seem to evade, rather than recognize, the new Daubert standard.

Given the Wisconsin appellate courts' disdain for Daubert, it is likely that, even if Avery were tried today in the Daubert era, the trial court would still allow the state to use its weird, non-science science at trial. That is, the EDTA test (even without a known method detection limit), the testimony about the burn site (even though entirely speculative at best), and the DNA test (even with its contamination and the analyst's disregard of testing protocol) may very well be deemed "the product of reliable principles and methods" under Daubert.

When there's a will (and a handy, flexible, ten-factor test for the court to apply), there's a way.

Chapter 5

THE WRONG-PERSON DEFENSE

"I did not do the crime, but I know who did."[1]

Prosecutors and judges like to say that a criminal trial is a "search for the truth."[2] And in some trials, the defendant not only wants to tell the jurors he's innocent, but he also wants to explain to them who actually committed the crime. And if trials really are about searching for the truth, who could possibly object to that?

THE TERESA HALBACH CASE

There were plenty of other suspects—other than Steven Avery and Brendan Dassey—for the Teresa Halbach murder. For example, *Making a Murderer* featured court testimony from several of Avery's relatives, including two men who were contradicted by other witnesses, who changed their stories from their previous statements, and who served as each other's alibi for the time surrounding the murder.[3] And there were also numerous people close to Halbach who law enforcement never even questioned—even though one investigator admitted that, in a homicide case, the murderer is often the one closest to, or even romantically involved with, the victim.

But although there were multiple alternative suspects who could have murdered Halbach, defense attorney Jerry Buting expressed his concern that, unless the defense could tell the jury "who we think did it," the jury would be reluctant to acquit Avery. Buting also complained that "the judge has really tied our hands on that."[4]

But what was Buting talking about? Of course a defendant can assert his innocence *and* show the jury who he thinks committed the crime, right? Telling the jury "who dunnit" is not only a good strategy—after all, no one likes to leave a case unresolved—but is also part of our constitutional right to present a defense, isn't it?

It is certainly reasonable to think that defendants have the right to present a wrong-person defense—so named because the defendant is arguing that the state charged the wrong person. And, in theory, the Constitution guarantees all of us the right to present a meaningful defense when the state accuses us of a crime.[5] But, as often happens, theory and practice fail to align in the criminal justice system. Consistent with the theme running throughout this book, courts have managed to turn yet another constitutional right into an empty promise.

What Buting was talking about was that, before trial, the prosecutor filed a motion asking the court "for an order prohibiting the defendant from arguing or otherwise introducing any evidence or inference [sic] that third parties other than Steven Avery, or co-defendant Brendan Dassey, are responsible for the intentional homicide of the victim, Teresa Halbach."[6]

In response to the state's motion, the judge ruled, "Should the defendant . . . intend to suggest that a third party . . . is responsible for any of the crimes charged, the defendant must notify the Court and the State at least thirty (30) days prior to the start of the trial . . . [and] will be subject to the standards . . . in *State v. Denny*, 120 Wis. 2d 614 (Ct. App. 1984)."[7]

THE DENNY TEST

The wrong-person defense—also known in Wisconsin as the third-party defense because the defendant is arguing that a third party, other than the defendant, committed the crime—is one of those defenses that sounds good in theory, but is actually very difficult to use. Before presenting such a defense to the jury, Wisconsin courts require the defendant to lay his cards on the table and satisfy the Denny three-part test by demonstrating (1) the third party's *motive* for committing the crime; (2) the third party's *opportunity* to commit the crime; and (3) a *direct connection* between the third party and the crime.[8] The Denny rule, as will soon become obvious, is a judicially created roadblock erected in front of the defendant for the purpose of ensuring his conviction and, in many cases, hiding the truth from the jury. (And, in Wisconsin's defense, several other states— including Florida, Illinois, Michigan, and Texas—have similar truth-suppressing rules that go by different names.)[9]

Let's begin with Denny's first requirement that the defendant has to demonstrate the third party's motive to commit the crime. This requirement is a purely arbitrary double standard, as the prosecutor is not required to prove the defendant's motive in order to charge or even convict him. Wisconsin courts even instruct juries that "[w]hile motive may be shown as a circumstance to aid in establishing the guilt of a defendant, *the State* is *not* required to prove *motive* on the part of a defendant in order to convict."[10]

In addition to being subjected to this higher burden and irrational double standard, a defendant also faces many practical problems when trying to prove a third party's motive. For example, how can a defendant possibly learn why the person committed the crime? Or what if the third party went on a psychopathic crime spree, and didn't even have a rational motive? Will the court still prevent the defendant from showing the jury who really committed the crime, just because the real perpetrator did not reveal, or simply didn't have, a motive?

The answer is yes. In fact, that is exactly what the trial court and, later, the appellate court said in the Halbach murder case: "[W]ithout evidence of motive, Avery's proffered third-party liability evidence fails. . . . The parties identified by Avery may have had the opportunity to commit the crime; however, Avery was unable to demonstrate that any of the named individuals had a motive to commit the alleged offenses against Halbach."[11]

But even if Avery could have demonstrated a third party's motive for murdering Halbach, the court probably still would have prevented him from using a third-party defense. A very recent Supreme Court of Wisconsin case demonstrates just how difficult it is to satisfy one of Denny's other prongs: showing the third party's opportunity to commit the crime.

To illustrate this, we must step aside from Avery's case and briefly examine the Wisconsin case of *State v. Wilson*.[12] There, the defendant appealed his murder-by-shooting conviction because the trial court would not let him argue that a third party, other than Wilson, committed the crime. On appeal, the state conceded that Wilson had properly demonstrated the third party's motive to murder the victim, and also established a direct connection between the third party and the crime. The only question for the court to decide was whether Wilson met Denny's second prong, demonstrating the third party's opportunity. The court framed the issue as "whether the alleged third-party perpetrator could have committed the crime in question."[13] The court added, "This often, but not always, amounts to a showing that the [third party] was *at the crime scene* or known to be in the vicinity when the crime was committed."[14]

The good news for defendant Wilson was that the third party who was the focus of his third-party defense was, in fact, "at the crime scene" at the precise time the victim was murdered. But the bad news for Wilson was that the court said a third party's presence at the crime scene is often, "but not always," evidence of opportunity. But how could a third party literally be at the crime scene yet not have the opportunity to kill the victim?

Here is where the court got hyper-technical (and hyper-creative) in order to affirm Wilson's conviction while denying him the right to present a third-party defense. The court first reasoned that Wilson had not offered a "direct shooter theory," but instead had argued that the third party drove the victim to the crime scene to be shot by someone else: the third party's hired gun.[15] Therefore, the court opined, the third party's actual presence at the crime scene failed to establish the *right kind* of opportunity. What kind of opportunity should defendant Wilson have established? The court said he should have demonstrated that the third party "had the means or access or ability" to hire the shooter.[16]

This is an excellent example of the disingenuous, moving-target legal gymnastics in which courts engage in order to deny defendants their right to present a wrong-person defense. First, the third party suspect (offered up by defendant Wilson) actually brought the victim to the eventual murder scene after the two of them left "an illegal after-hours club operated by" the third party's brother.[17] Isn't that enough to show that the third party "had the means or access or ability" to hire some low-rent hack to pull the trigger? Apparently not. The court would have preferred that Wilson provide the third party's "telephone records" to prove that he arranged the hit, as well as the names of people the third party may have employed as "the shooter or shooters."[18]

This so-called legal reasoning is, of course, absurd. First, the court fails to explain how, exactly, Wilson could have possibly gained access to the third party's "telephone records" or the names of "the shooter or shooters" hired by the third party. And even if Wilson had somehow obtained such phone records, the court would have simply dismissed such evidence for failing to demonstrate anything about the *content* of the calls that were placed. Similarly, even if Wilson had furnished a list of potential shooters, the court would have simply declared the information to be purely speculative and, therefore, insufficient to satisfy the Denny test.

Second, and more important, the court ignores that the third party would have been contacting and hiring people for the purpose of plotting and carrying out a murder; therefore, the third party would have gone to great lengths to hide such information in order to avoid leaving a paper trail and being caught. This, of course, made it practically impossible for Wilson to have obtained the information required by the court.

Avery's Halbach case and *State v. Wilson* demonstrate how incredibly difficult it is for a defendant to hurdle Denny's three-part test and use a wrong-person defense at trial. Worse yet, Avery's first case—the Beerntsen rape case—proves that Wisconsin's rigid, irrational Denny rule often operates to hide the truth and convict the innocent.

AVERY, BEERNTSEN, AND GREGORY ALLEN

In the Beerntsen case, *Making a Murderer* focused on Deputy Gene Kusche's sketch of Avery and how the sheriff's department's tunnel vision led to Beerntsen's misidentification of Avery as the perpetrator. But the documentary also discussed how, before Avery's trial, the Manitowoc Police Department told the Manitowoc Sheriff's Department that a third party, Gregory Allen, was likely the real perpetrator. This aspect of the documentary nicely demonstrates a practical problem with the wrong-person defense: in most cases, the defendant is not even aware of such a defense because law enforcement never bothered to explore—or in some cases even concealed— evidence of the third party's guilt.

This issue came to a head in Avery's 1997 appeal of his conviction for the Beerntsen rape. By 1997, Avery's defense team had reason to believe that, when Avery was being prosecuted in the mid-1980s, the sheriffs actually had evidence that would have pointed to the third party's guilt. In the appeal, Avery's appellate lawyer argued that the sheriffs had been "aware of a man in Sheboygan County who matched the description of the perpetrator. . . ."[19] Further, this man "was under investigation with regard to [the Beerntsen] case."[20] Finally, thanks to advances in DNA testing, Avery also had evidence that the DNA of a third party, other than Avery and the victim, was found under the victim's fingernails. (At this time, however, the defense could only say that the DNA did not belong to Avery or Beerntsen; the defense did not yet know that the DNA belonged specifically to Gregory Allen.) All of this, Avery argued, constituted a viable wrong-person defense, and he should, therefore, be entitled to a new trial.

Once again, the Denny rule reared its ugly head and operated to suppress evidence of innocence while ensuring—or, in the case of this appeal, preserving—a wrongful conviction. The appellate court held that Avery's third-party guilt theory was "far too vague to demonstrate that Avery would be entitled to a new trial."[21] Denny, the court held, "requires the defendant to offer proof of motive, opportunity, and a direct connection between the third party and the crime. . . . Taking all of Avery's facts as true, they fail this test."[22]

At the time of this 1997 appeal, it is unclear what more Avery could have done. He had denied that he attacked Beerntsen. He had presented sixteen alibi witnesses placing him far from the crime scene. The state had no physical evidence linking him to the crime. The victim's description of the perpetrator did not match Avery in several respects, including eye color. The victim's in-court identification of Avery as the perpetrator was based on highly suggestive, pretrial identification procedures. And now, thanks to new DNA evidence and new evidence that the sheriffs had concealed at the time of his jury trial, Avery was able to point the finger at a third party. Despite all of this, Denny's three-part test is so rigid and irrational that the appellate court would not even give Avery a new trial, let alone release him from prison.

THE POLICY BEHIND DENNY

All of this raises the question: what underlying policy could possibly justify Wisconsin's conviction-affirming, truth-suppressing Denny test? It is important to remember that the defendant who offers a wrong-person defense does not actually put the third party on trial. Therefore, there is no risk that, during the trial, the third party could be convicted of the crime with which the defendant is charged. Consequently, even if the defendant is mistaken about who, in fact, committed the crime, only one question remains for the jury to answer and that is whether there is reasonable doubt that *the defendant* committed the crime.

Without any risk that a third party could be wrongfully convicted at the defendant's trial, the government attempts to justify the Denny rule as follows: the three-part test "ensures that proffered evidence meets the necessary evidentiary threshold before it is admitted while, at the same time, guarding the constitutional rights of defendants."[23]

First, this justification was uttered by the Supreme Court of Wisconsin in 2015, long after Avery's defense team proved that a third party, Gregory Allen, had actually raped Beerntsen, and that the Denny rule had failed miserably in "guarding the constitutional rights" of Steven Avery. And second, if read closely, what does the court's justification even say? It really says nothing of substance; rather, the court is merely declaring that it will continue to use the Denny test because it likes it.

Once in a while, though, it is actually possible to get a straight answer out of a judge. Avery's trial judge in the Halbach murder case was surprisingly forthcoming about the real reason behind the Denny rule: "One can only imagine how much longer this six-week trial would have lasted had the court granted Avery's request to introduce third-party liability evidence. . . ."[24]

So what is the lesson in all of this? Despite the government's claim that trials are a "search for the truth,"[25] defendants generally will not be permitted to "waste" valuable court time by presenting evidence that a third party, other than the defendant, committed the crime. In other words, truth takes a backseat to ensuring shorter workdays for the judiciary.

AN ALTERNATIVE TO THE WRONG-PERSON DEFENSE

Jerry Buting and Dean Strang were prevented from using the wrong-person defense at Avery's trial in the Halbach murder case; therefore, they were not allowed to point the finger at a specific third party as the murderer. But there was an alternative defense: "A common trial tactic of defense lawyers is to discredit the caliber of the [police] investigation or the [prosecutor's] decision to charge the defendant. . . ."[26]

This alternative defense argues that the defendant doesn't know the identity of the real perpetrator—and certainly doesn't have any evidence of that person's motive, opportunity, or direct involvement—because the police did such a horrible job of investigating the case. And because of their shoddy investigation, such information was never obtained and is now lost forever. Further, the argument continues, their shoddy investigation led to the defendant being wrongfully prosecuted for the crime.[27] The US Supreme Court has described this defense as follows:

> [T]he defense could have attacked the investigation as shoddy. . . .
> [The evidence] would have raised opportunities to attack not only the probative value of crucial physical evidence and the circumstances in which it was found, but the thoroughness and even the good faith of the investigation as well. . . .
>
> [T]he defense could have . . . attacked the reliability of the investigation in *failing even to consider [a third party's] possible guilt*. . . . [I]ndications of conscientious police work will enhance proba-

tive force [of the government's evidence at trial] and slovenly work will diminish it. . . .

[T]he defense could have laid the foundation for a vigorous argument that the police had been guilty of negligence. . . . Since *the police admittedly never treated [any third party] as a suspect*, the defense could . . . throw the reliability of the investigation into doubt and to sully the credibility of [the] Detective. . . .

[The evidence] would simply have underscored the unreliability of the investigation and complemented the defense's attack on the *failure to treat [others] as a suspect.* . . . The jury would have been entitled to find that the investigation was limited by the police's uncritical readiness to accept the story . . . [and] that the lead police detective who testified was either less than wholly candid or less than fully informed. . . .[28]

Given the tunnel vision of the Manitowoc Sheriff's Department, as well as the other law enforcement agencies involved in the Halbach murder investigation, this defense was tailor-made for Avery's case. In fact, Avery's defense team did an excellent job of exposing the government's investigation as "shoddy" and "slovenly." Better still, the defense was able to "sully the credibility" of several law enforcement agents, and also exposed them as being "less than wholly candid" when testifying under oath.[29] And all of this was done in the context of showing that the government failed to even consider, let alone investigate, the guilt of any third party. In a sense, then, despite the prosecutor's best efforts to completely shut them down, Avery's defense team was still able to use a watered-down version of the third-party defense.

But even with this defense, Avery was convicted. There are at least two reasons for this. First, this alternative defense of attacking the police investigation is not as good as the third-party defense itself—at least not in Avery's particular case. Avery's jury wanted to know who specifically murdered Halbach, but the judge prevented the defense team from attempting to answer that burning question. And second, any defense theory that attacks the police—especially when that attack goes beyond accusations of mere negligence to accusations of a frame job—is risky business in government-loving communities like Manitowoc, Wisconsin.

Avery's defense lawyer Dean Strang even conceded, "No sane lawyer looks forward to presenting an argument to a jury that the police framed his client."[30] And he had good reason to feel that way. Consider, for example, the prosecutors' outrage—whether feigned or real—when the defense turned the tables and targeted the cops. Ken Kratz called the defense "deplorable"; Norm Gahn, appearing distraught, described the cops as "good, solid citizens; good, decent men."[31] And the news media bought into this police-are-the-good-guys refrain. One reporter even asked Dean Strang at a press conference how their defense of Steven Avery might negatively impact the individual law enforcement agents and their children.

This hero-like view of law enforcement is one that the government seeks to cultivate in us at an early age. (Remember Deputy Friendly in grade school?) And once ingrained, this mindset is hard to break for most people. For example, the Manitowoc Sheriff's Department was largely responsible for Avery's wrongful conviction in the Beerntsen rape. They ignored the Manitowoc Police Department's warning that Gregory Allen, not Avery, was the real perpetrator, which not only cost Avery eighteen years of his life, but also permitted Allen to remain free and victimize more women before he was eventually caught. Yet, despite all of this widely publicized information, the jury in the Halbach case was still comfortable ignoring law enforcement's shoddy investigation, tunnel vision, and even flip-flopping testimony. Why? Because the cops are "good, solid citizens; good, decent men."

This hero worship of law enforcement apparently survives even after a law enforcement agency proves, at minimum, that it is capable of incompetence. As the prosecutors warned the defense team before the Halbach trial, when the defense dares to criticize the government and its agents, it does so at its peril.

Chapter 6

INTERROGATIONS AND FALSE CONFESSIONS

"What I can't figure out is why you said all this shit if it's not true!"

—Barb Tadych, Brendan Dassey's mother

"Cuz I'm stupid, I told you!"

—Brendan Dassey

Brendan Dassey played a significant role in *Making a Murderer*. Not only did his alleged confession impact Steven Avery's trial defense in numerous ways, but it also resulted in Dassey's own conviction for being a "party to" the murder of Teresa Halbach.

In multiple statements to law enforcement, Dassey painted a vivid picture of Halbach's murder—the crime in which he claimed to have participated. The problem, though, is that his story was not supported by any of the physical evidence. In fact, his story—a tale of an incredibly violent and bloody rape, torture, throat slashing, and murder that took place in Avery's trailer—was completely *contradicted* by all of the physical evidence.

So given this, why would the jury believe Dassey's story? And even before that, why would Dassey make up, and then admit to, something he didn't do? And going back even further, why would Dassey talk to the cops in the first place?

"YOU HAVE THE RIGHT TO REMAIN SILENT"

We have all heard the popular Miranda warning so many times that we can probably repeat it verbatim.[1] In nearly every crime drama to hit the airwaves, the arresting officer sternly warns the suspect:

> You have the right to remain silent; anything you say can and will be used against you in a court of law; you have the right to consult with a lawyer before questioning and to have a lawyer present with you during questioning; if you cannot afford to hire a lawyer, one will be appointed to represent you. . . .[2]

The idea behind these warnings was to provide suspects with some protection against the intimidating, coercive, and overwhelming nature of an in-custody police interrogation. And although it was not explicitly discussed in *Making a Murderer*, before one of his multiple interrogations "Dassey was read his Miranda rights and signed a waiver."[3] But why, after hearing this stern and intimidating warning, would Dassey waive his rights and risk talking to law enforcement? Why wouldn't he instead "remain silent," or at least "consult with a lawyer before questioning"?

The answer is that real-life cops like the ones in *Making a Murderer* do not deliver Miranda warnings the way fictional cops do in television dramas. In fact, real-life cops are trained to *avoid* reading Miranda whenever possible. And the law is on their side. The police are not required to read a suspect his Miranda rights unless both of the following things are true: (1) the police are going to question the suspect, and (2) the suspect is in custody.[4]

Given this, the easiest way to avoid reading Miranda is simply to question the suspect when he is not yet in custody. How? The police can go to the suspect's home, work, or school to question him there. If the police don't want to question the suspect at one of these locations, they can simply "invite" the suspect to "voluntarily" come to the police station—often in a police squad car. Each of these situations is, of course, the functional equivalent of being in custody, as it is highly unlikely the suspect would simply get up and walk away in response to police questioning. Yet the police will pretend (and later testify in court, if necessary) that the suspect was free to leave at any time and, therefore, the police were not required to read Miranda.[5]

It really is that simple. In fact, that is exactly what happened to Dassey. The sequence of events is recited in his appellate court decision as follows:

> On February 27, 2006, law enforcement officers conducted a witness interview of Dassey at his high school and a second videotaped interview at the Two Rivers Police Department. . . . On March 1 . . . officers retrieved Dassey from school for a videotaped interview. . . . Dassey made several inculpatory statements over the course of the three-hour interview, such that he now was viewed as a suspect.[6]

While the court's dates are correct (though incomplete), its conclusions are flat-out wrong. On February 27, 2006, Brendan Dassey was not the subject of a "witness interview." Rather, government agents Mark Wiegert and Tom Fassbender were interrogating him as a suspect. But because they employed the tactic described earlier—first questioning Dassey at school rather than at the police station—they could claim that he was not in custody and was not entitled to Miranda warnings. And because they knew that the highly compliant, learning-disabled, sixteen-year-old child would not simply get up and walk away, they saw no risk in beginning their interrogation as follows:

> You're free to go at any time you want. . . . Um and I, I would really appreciate if you would just kinda relax and open up with us. We're not here ta jump in your face or get into ya or anything like that. I know that may have happened before and stuff like that, we're, we're not here to do that. We're here more ta maybe let you talk or talk to you a little about how you've been feeling lately and stuff.[7]

But after this pleasant and reassuring opening—complete with feigned concern about how Dassey had "been feeling lately and stuff"—Wiegert and Fassbender quickly got to the business of interrogating Dassey not as a witness, but as a suspect in the Halbach murder case. They told Dassey,

You're a kid, you know we got, we've got people back at the sheriff's department, district attorney's office, and their [sic] lookin' at this now saying there's no way that Brendan Dassey was out there and didn't see something. They're talking about trying to link Brendan Dassey with this event. . . . [T]hey're saying that Brendan had something to do with it or the cover up of it which would mean Brendan Dassey *could potentially be facing charges for that.*[8]

So, quite obviously, the cops viewed Dassey as a suspect, not a witness, as early as his February 27, 2006, interrogation at his school, which occurred before the March 1, 2006, interrogation video shown on *Making a Murderer.*

But eventually, somewhere during the course of their numerous contacts and interviews, the cops *did* read Dassey his rights. Given that, why would Dassey continue to talk to them after he was told he could remain silent or even consult with an attorney? There are several reasons.

First, by the time Wiegert and Fassbender finally read Dassey his rights, they had already obtained several statements in their earlier, so-called "witness interview" at the school. The cat, therefore, was already out of the bag by the time Dassey first heard the Miranda warning. That is, Dassey likely viewed the in-station interrogation as a mere continuation of the earlier questioning. Having already been softened up, he simply did not appreciate the grave harm that could come to him by continuing to talk to his interrogators.

But second, and most significantly, when the police actually do read a suspect his Miranda rights, they have developed numerous tactics to induce the suspect to waive, rather than invoke, his right to remain silent and to consult with a lawyer.

In our recent article, Anthony Domanico, Lawrence White, and I explored these police tactics by examining actual, recorded police interrogations in Wisconsin. To begin, we asked, how often do suspects in custody waive their Miranda rights? It turns out that Dassey was not alone in his eagerness to talk. In our study, 93 percent (27 of 29 suspects) waived their rights and talked to police.[9] A similar percentage exists nationwide.[10]

Other social science studies are consistent with our finding: the vast majority of suspects will waive their rights and talk, likely thinking that if they remain silent or, worse yet, "lawyer up," they will appear guilty.[11] And interestingly, the Miranda warning itself does nothing to dispel this fear. The warning does inform the suspect that his statements may be used against him; however, it does not inform him that his silence, or his request for an attorney, may *not* be used against him.[12] In light of the Miranda warning's incomplete information, the typical suspect's eagerness to talk—or, rather, his fear of remaining silent—is understandable.[13]

And there are other reasons that suspects waive their rights and talk—often to their great detriment. First, in our study of actual, recorded police interrogations we found that most suspects probably did not understand the warnings in the first place. The Wisconsin version of the Miranda warning requires a tenth-grade reading level to understand, yet the reading ability of most criminal suspects falls well below that mark.[14] And because the cops *want* the suspect to talk—in many investigations, the cops need the statement or they won't even have a case against the suspect—the interrogators in our sample made virtually no effort to ensure that suspects understood their rights.[15]

Here, once again, Dassey was typical: his reading ability was at the fourth-grade level, leaving him little hope of understanding the Miranda warnings rattled off by his interrogators. Further, Dassey's interrogators, like the police in our study, made no effort to ensure that he understood the rights he was about to waive.[16]

But to say the police generally make no effort to ensure that suspects understand their rights is actually a gross understatement. In our analysis of recorded police interrogations in Wisconsin, we found that the police actually *minimized* the significance of the Miranda warning.[17] This conveys to the suspect that these rights are not important, but rather are just a formality that must quickly be addressed before getting down to business. The result, of course, is that suspects are more likely to waive, rather than invoke, their rights.

For example, one interrogator in our study said, "I'm going to read you your rights real quick; it's part of the formality."[18] Such minimization occurred in nearly half of the interrogations we examined.[19] And when that particular interrogator told the suspect his rights would be read "real quick," he wasn't kidding. In our sample of twenty-nine Wisconsin interrogations, the interrogators spoke 31 percent faster when giving Miranda warnings than they did during the parts of the interrogation before and after the warnings.[20] And speed matters: it is well known that when an interrogator's speaking rate increases, the suspect's comprehension of what is being said decreases.[21]

Not surprisingly, this minimization of the Miranda rights played a role in Dassey's interrogation as well. In order to induce a quick waiver and to move on to the questioning, the interrogators said, "But before we ask any question Brendan, um, I have to read you your rights. It's just what we have to do. . . ."[22]

But far worse than minimizing Dassey's rights, his interrogators did two additional things. First, after telling him that he had the right to consult with a lawyer before answering the questions they were about to ask him, they quickly took that option off the table: "We have no way of getting you a lawyer."[23] And second, they did not even give him the option of invoking any of the rights they had quickly read to him. Instead, they simply gave him one option: to waive. They read from their preprinted form and asked Dassey to agree that,

> I have read the above statement of my rights[.] I understand what my rights are, *I am willing to answer questions and to make statements. I do not want a lawyer.* I understand and know what I am doing. No promises or threats have been made to me and no pressure of any kind has been used against me.[24]

Dassey, of course, timidly accepted the only choice presented to him: skip the lawyer, answer the questions, and make a statement.[25]

But while all of this Miranda trickery explains why Dassey decided to talk to the cops in the first place, the question still remains: once he started talking, why would he ever admit to something he didn't do?

THE INTERROGATION

Just as the police have tactics for getting suspects to waive, rather than invoke, their Miranda rights, they also have tactics for getting suspects to say what they (the police) want to hear.

To begin, police interrogations are a guilt-presumptive process.[26] Contrary to what the police say, interrogations are not searches for the truth. Instead, the interrogators go into the interrogation room already believing that the suspect is guilty, and then employ numerous tactics to get the suspect to say things that corroborate the interrogators' preexisting theory of guilt.

For example, in Dassey's case, the police claim to have learned from a young relative of his that Dassey lost weight, was depressed, and was crying after Halbach's disappearance. This, it turns out, was all they needed to leap to the conclusion that Dassey was involved in her murder. How was that information sufficient? Because, they concluded, the guilt was eating away at Dassey's soul; there simply could be no other explanation for why a teenage boy would be depressed, crying, and losing weight.

Of course, we know from *Making a Murderer* that Dassey was intentionally losing weight because other kids were calling him fat, and he was depressed and crying because his first-ever girlfriend broke up with him. And a simple inquiry by the cops would have uncovered this, but they appeared to have no interest in such information. (Despite their reassurances to Dassey, they were never interested in talking to him "about how you've been feeling lately and stuff.") Again, interrogations are a guilt-presumptive process, and such information would have contradicted their theory that Dassey was experiencing crushing guilt for helping Avery murder Halbach.

But even if the police made up their minds ahead of time that Dassey was guilty, what could they possibly have done to get him to *agree* that he was guilty if, in fact, he was innocent? The police unleashed several interrogation tactics on the unsuspecting, intellectually impaired, depressed, and scared teenager. Among these tactics was the highly effective interrogation strategy known as minimization.[27] That is, in addition to minimizing the significance of a suspect's Miranda rights, the police also minimize the seriousness of the allegation itself. In this context, however, their goal is not to get a waiver of rights, but rather a confession to the crime.

The minimization strategy begins by offering the suspect two, and only two, choices: (1) you committed this crime, you meant to do it, and you're an unforgivable monster; or (2) you sort of did this, but you really didn't mean to do it, and someone or something else is really to blame for it. (The suspect's complete innocence, of course, is not presented as an option.) If the suspect accepts these as his two choices, then the second option is far more attractive. However, what the suspect does not realize is that the interrogators are indifferent as to which option he chooses. From their perspective, option number two is just as incriminating as option number one.

With Dassey, interrogators Mark Wiegert and Tom Fassbender employed this strategy beautifully. They first made it very clear that Dassey's actual innocence, and complete lack of involvement in the murder, was simply not an option. They repeatedly told him that they already knew what happened, his denials were lies, and he just needed to admit to them what they already knew. As Lawrence White—the false confession expert in *Making a Murderer*—explained, even though Wiegert and Fassbender pretended to demand "the truth," what they were really saying was, "don't tell us *that*; tell us something else—something that fits [our] theory of the crime."[28]

Wiegert and Fassbender then made sure that Dassey had an "out" by making the second option very attractive. They created a scenario of his involvement in the murder that minimized his moral blame. During the video-recorded interrogation in *Making a Murderer*, they often referred to what Avery had done, and "what he made you do," thus shifting blame away from Dassey and onto Avery as the primary actor.[29]

The interrogators continually emphasized that, if Dassey admitted to his supporting role in the incident, everything would be okay because none of this was his fault. They also assured him that, in addition to not being assigned any moral blame, option number two also came with tremendous leniency:

> I'm a father that has a kid your age too. I wanna be here for you. There's nothing I'd like more than to come over and give you a hug cuz I know you're hurtin'. . . . Talk about it, we're not just going to let you high and dry. . . . *I promise I will not let you high and dry, I'll stand behind you.*[30]

These minimization techniques—placing moral blame on someone or something else, promising leniency, etc.—are highly effective in getting even innocent suspects to confess. However, they don't always work. And when the suspect refuses to accept either of the two choices offered to him, the interrogators can look like foolish amateurs. This is what happened when the cops interrogated Steven Avery.

In a video-recorded interrogation shown in *Making a Murderer*, Avery's interrogators used the same minimization strategy. They began by presenting Avery with the formulaic false dichotomy: (1) you planned to kill Teresa Halbach, and you're an irredeemable monster; or (2) you killed her but it was a mistake, you didn't really mean to do it, and if you admit your mistake your family will understand. The interrogators even found a way to minimize Avery's moral responsibility, telling him that it really wasn't his fault. They told him, it was his eighteen years of wrongful incarceration (for the Beerntsen rape) that screwed him up psychologically. That, the interrogators offered, was the reason Avery made the mistake of killing Halbach.

This tactic didn't work on Avery, who realized he had a third option: absolute innocence. And in light of Avery's realization, the interrogators looked silly. The idea of someone "mistakenly" shooting a person multiple times and then burning her body is absurd—although, admittedly, the interrogators' angle of blaming Avery's eighteen years of wrongful incarceration was fairly creative.

But despite their failure in Avery's interrogation, the cops were still batting .500 as their minimization strategy worked to near perfection on Dassey. Dassey even truly believed Wiegert's and Fassbender's promises of leniency: after essentially confessing to a horrific murder, Dassey asked them how much longer their interview would last, as he wanted to be returned to school by 1:29 p.m. to turn in his project that was due at 1:30 p.m. Dassey soon learned, however, that his interrogators' promises not to leave him "high and dry," but instead to "stand behind" him, were outright lies.

Brendan Dassey is not the first real-life suspect to be victimized by well-honed interrogation tactics. Additionally, the effectiveness of the minimization strategy has been replicated in controlled studies as well. In one realistic simulation, for example, 43 percent of suspects (who were known by the researchers to be innocent of the accusation) falsely confessed as a result of the interrogators' minimization tactics.[31] The reality is that when suspects believe it is in their best interest to adopt the interrogators' theory of the case—also known as option number two—many of them will do so, even when doing so means falsely confessing.

With regard to Dassey, it is not at all surprising that he would accept option number two and falsely confess to having some involvement in the Halbach murder. The people most likely to fall prey to minimization tactics are those who are young, are highly compliant with authority figures, have little or no experience dealing with the police, are intellectually impaired, and are depressed.[32] At the time of his interrogation, Dassey fit all of those classifications. Lawrence White summed it up this way:

> [T]here are reasons to believe that Brendan Dassey's statements may not be wholly reliable or truly voluntary. Brendan is a vulnerable individual due to his low intelligence, poor memory skills, and passive demeanor. The police repeatedly pressured Brendan to provide them with details that conformed to their theory of the crime. Brendan's statements were often inconsistent, ambivalent, and self-contradictory. In sum, there are many reasons to question the trustworthiness and voluntariness of Brendan Dassey's so-called "confession."[33]

Getting Dassey to confess to a crime he probably never even witnessed, let alone participated in, was among the easiest things that Wiegert and Fassbender had to do that entire day.

CONFESSIONS AND JURIES

The incomplete and confusing language of the Miranda warnings, combined with the way the police deliver those warnings, explains why most suspects decide to talk instead of remaining silent or asking for a lawyer. And the numerous interrogation strategies, including the minimization technique used against Dassey, explain why suspects think it is in their best interest to admit some involvement in the crime, even when they are completely innocent. But this still does not explain why a jury would *believe* a confession like Dassey's—

a confession that was unsupported, and even contradicted, by all of the physical evidence.

Even more interesting, Dassey never really affirmatively "confessed" to anything of value. It is true that, when the interrogators continually prodded him to "be honest," he did dream up many details on his own—including incredibly bloody details. But again, that story was proved false by the physical evidence. In reality, the only valuable piece of information that came from Dassey's interrogation was that Halbach was shot in the head. But on closer examination, this piece of information did *not* come from Dassey.

In the video-recorded interrogation shown in *Making a Murderer*, the interrogators repeatedly asked Dassey, "What happened to her head?"[34] Hoping that Dassey would admit to *shooting* her in the head, Wiegert and Fassbender impatiently sat through his multiple guesses. But Dassey struggled to correctly guess the answer they wanted to hear. He first guessed that Avery "cut off her hair," then "punched her" head, and then "cut her" throat.[35] None of these, however, satisfied the interrogators. Instead, their frustration grew because Dassey's guesses were contradicted by the physical evidence in the case.

What happened next, as defense lawyer Jerry Buting explained, is that interrogator Wiegert, in his impatience, blew "the one piece of secret evidence that could have corroborated Brendan Dassey's story by *feeding it to him himself.*"[36] After Dassey's multiple, incorrect guesses about what happened to the victim's head, the exchange went like this:

> Interrogator: I'm just gonna come out and ask ya, who *shot her* in the head?
> Dassey: He did. (Referring to Avery.)
> Interrogator (frustrated): Then why didn't you tell us that?
> Dassey: Cuz I couldn't think of it.[37]

So not only was Dassey's entire tale contradicted by the physical evidence—for example, not one drop of Halbach's blood or a single spec of her DNA was found in the trailer—but his so-called confession really wasn't even a confession. Rather, the police fed the critical piece of information to Dassey—within the structure of their highly effective minimization strategy—and Dassey agreed to the information they fed him: Avery *shot* Halbach in the head.

The problem for Dassey, though, is that the jury still viewed this as *his* confession. And, as Dassey later learned at trial, "When the state charges an individual with a crime, one of the most compelling pieces of evidence it can present to a jury is the defendant's alleged confession. Confessions are powerful evidence due to the commonly held belief that such statements, made against one's own interest, simply *must be true.*"[38] Conversely stated, "The idea that an individual would [falsely] confess to a crime, particularly a horrific crime such as murder or rape, without being subject to physical torture, runs counter to the intuition of most people."[39] In fact, when used at trial, "the jury is likely to treat the confession as more probative of the defendant's guilt than any other evidence."[40]

To explore the incredible power of confession evidence, Danielle Chojnacki, Lawrence White, and I set out to discover what, exactly, jury-eligible citizens believe about false confessions. We surveyed a very large sample size of participants, and quickly found out why confessions carry such great weight with juries.

First, 49 percent of our study participants agreed—with only 5 percent disagreeing and 46 percent being uncertain—that properly trained individuals "can detect lying by observing a person's body language."[41] And, in Dassey's trial, a law enforcement officer testified that, during his interrogation, Dassey's head was down and he was withdrawn. This officer also testified that, in his training and experience, such body language constituted evidence of an inner struggle due to guilt. And if that wasn't clear enough, the jury also watched the video where the interrogators repeatedly called Dassey a liar whenever he gave an answer that was not consistent with his guilt.

The reality, however, is that police are *not* able to detect whether the person is having an inner struggle or is simply highly uncomfortable. Further, controlled studies demonstrate that individuals trained in detecting deception are not effective at distinguishing truthful statements from false statements.[42] And the individuals who go through such training may not be getting their money's worth: when attempting to identify false statements, they perform no better than pure chance.[43] But unfortunately, because Dassey did not have an expert witness to explain this at trial, the jury, much like the survey respondents in our study, believed that the police are human lie detectors, that Dassey's initial denials were false, and that his eventual confession, even though largely fed to him by the police, was true.

Second, 73 percent of our study participants believed that an innocent person would either "never confess" to a crime, or would confess only after "strenuous pressure" to do so.[44] And in Dassey's trial, the jury saw the interrogation video where the police used the opposite tactic. That is, instead of using "strenuous pressure"— a tactic known as maximization—Dassey's interrogators used the softer but equally effective strategy of minimization. As we saw, Dassey's interrogators knew that minimization was the preferred method for dealing with a depressed, highly compliant, learning disabled, sixteen-year-old child.

The problem, then, is that Dassey's jurors, much like the participants in our study, simply did not appreciate the power of these softer, subtler interrogation tactics to induce false confessions. Yet these tactics are just as effective as the "strenuous pressure" that jurors *do* associate with false confessions. In fact, in Dassey's case, minimization was far more effective than any threatening, maximization tactics could have ever been. So once again, without an expert witness to explain this at trial, the jury was left believing that Dassey's initial denials were false, and that his eventual confession was true.

THE TRUTH WILL SET YOU FREE?

What if an innocent person wants to waive his Miranda rights, talk to the police, and adamantly deny any involvement in the crime? In this situation, the suspect is better off talking to the police, isn't he?

The reality is that people do want to talk. And the police know this, so they will often entice suspects by telling them this is your "only opportunity" or your "last chance" to tell "your side" of the story. But, as is the case with much of what the police tell us citizens, this too is a lie. First, it is the rare case that a suspect could avoid arrest by telling her side of what happened. Remember that interrogations are a guilt-presumptive event. The police do not want to talk to the suspect to determine *what* happened; rather, they want the suspect to say things that confirm what the police think they already know.

And second, the police interrogation likely won't be the "only opportunity" or the "last chance" for the suspect to talk. Any prosecutor would happily listen to or read a suspect-turned-defendant's statement after the case is charged, and every jury would be eager to hear what the defendant has to say at trial.

But even though this common police inducement is false, it meshes nicely with the innocent suspect's belief that the truth will set him free—or, in the pre-arrest situation, keep him free. But the reality is that even when a suspect is actually innocent, resists the interrogation tactics designed to get him to confess, and adamantly denies any wrongdoing, his words can simply be cherry-picked—or even outright fabricated—and then used against him at trial as evidence of his guilt.

For an example of this, we must now leave Brendan Dassey's interrogation and travel back in time about twenty years to Steven Avery's first case, where he was charged with the rape and attempted murder of Penny Beerntsen. This is a case where we know, for certain, that Avery was innocent: in addition to his sixteen alibi witnesses, serial rapist Gregory Allen's DNA—not Avery's—was found in the samples taken from the victim's body. (This is why even the prosecutor joined in Avery's request for freedom eighteen years after his wrongful conviction.)

Yet despite Avery's actual innocence, his statement to the police at the time of his arrest was still used against him, at trial, as evidence of his guilt. Here is what the appellate court wrote in 1987 when denying Avery's first appeal:

> We also note that [Beerntsen's] identification of Avery was *corroborated by Avery's statements* at the time of his arrest. Although the testimony [at trial] indicated that the police told him *only* that he was under arrest "for attempted first degree murder," Avery told his wife [who was present at the time of his arrest] that "they say I murdered *a woman*" and asked [the police] where "*the lady*" lived. Since no one had mentioned the fact that the victim was a woman, the jury could properly deem Avery's statements to be inculpatory, corroborating the identification.[45]

Now, it is possible that the cops suffered from faulty memories at Avery's trial. When arresting Avery, maybe they really told him that he was under arrest "for attempted first-degree murder *of Penny Beerntsen*," and then forgot the last part of this sentence when they testified about it in court. That would explain why Avery referred to the victim as "a woman" at the time he was being arrested.

But let's assume that everything the appellate court wrote is exactly what was said when the cops arrested Avery. In that case, the prosecutor successfully used an innocent man's statement against him as evidence of his guilt. The argument, as the appellate court stated, takes the form of a question: how else could Avery have known that the victim was a woman unless he actually committed the crime?

The answer is innocent and simple. Even if the police did not mention that the victim was a woman, Avery probably assumed so because in his mind—whether correct or incorrect—murder victims are typically women. And when he asked "where the lady lived," he was obviously hoping to clear up the situation by offering his alibi to the police, thereby proving that he was nowhere near the lady's home (which he obviously, but incorrectly, assumed was the crime scene). Yet, despite these innocent explanations for his statement— and despite his *actual* innocence—the government twisted his words and used them as evidence of his guilt not only at trial, but also throughout the appeals process.

The point, of course, is that speaking to the police, or even within earshot of the police, is fraught with peril.[46] In that respect, the Miranda warning, despite its numerous flaws, is correct: *anything* you say can and will be used against you in a court of law.

Chapter 7

TRUTH, DOUBT, AND THE BURDEN OF PROOF

"The State ain't gotta prove nothin'. An innocent person always has to prove his self."

—Steven Avery

How could the jury have convicted Steven Avery of the Penny Beerntsen rape when there was no physical evidence against him and he had sixteen alibi witnesses placing him far away from the crime scene? How could the jury have convicted Avery of the Teresa Halbach murder when the state had big problems with crucial pieces of evidence, and it was even likely that Halbach was murdered elsewhere and then transported *to* Avery's property? And how could the jury have convicted Brendan Dassey as a "party to" Halbach's murder when his alleged confession was contradicted by all of the physical evidence?

There is no single answer to any one of these questions, although sometimes a very big contributing factor can easily be identified. For example, what most heavily contributed to Avery's conviction in the Beerntsen case was the initial show-up identification procedure, which set off a chain of events culminating in Beerntsen's in-court identification. Similarly, the factor that most heavily contributed to Dassey's conviction as a "party to" Halbach's murder was the government's use of coercive interrogation tactics known to produce false confessions.

But underlying and contributing to all three of the convictions in *Making a Murderer* is the surprisingly low, and unconstitutional, burden of proof in Wisconsin criminal courts. To appreciate this problem, we first need to understand three interrelated concepts: the presumption of innocence, proof by the preponderance of the evidence, and proof beyond a reasonable doubt.

THE PRESUMPTION OF INNOCENCE

Criminal cases are supposed to begin with the presumption of innocence. Wisconsin jurors, including the jurors in the Halbach murder trial, are instructed as follows: "Defendants are not required to prove their innocence. The law presumes every person charged with the commission of an offense to be innocent."[1]

Despite this high-minded language, however, many defendants are convicted before their jury is even sworn. For example, when Avery's written juror questionnaires came back, defense lawyer Jerry Buting was dismayed that only one out of 130 prospective jurors believed Avery might be innocent.

Prospective jurors are also questioned about the presumption of innocence in court, during the jury selection process known as *voir dire*. During *voir dire*, many would-be jurors will openly admit they believe the defendant is guilty merely because he was accused, arrested, or criminally charged.

This is how a typical jury selection, or *voir dire*, plays out in court:

> **Defense Counsel**: . . . The evidence will show that my client . . . was in fact *arrested* by the police in this case. Does the fact that he was *arrested* make anyone think that he must be guilty of some crime?
>
> **Potential Juror #7**: Yes. If the police arrested him, there was good reason.
>
> **Defense Counsel**: Thank you for responding. Now, the judge told you earlier today that everyone charged with a crime is presumed innocent, and it is for you the jurors, and not the police or anyone else, to determine whether he is guilty. Do you still think that my client is guilty merely because he was arrested?

Potential Juror #7: Yes, if he was arrested, he did something wrong. That's just how I feel.

Defense Counsel: Do you think you could set that feeling aside, presume him innocent, and judge this case on the evidence?

Potential Juror #7. I'd really like to try, but I don't think I'd be fair. The police aren't going to waste their time with innocent people. I believe that the arrest alone shows that he's guilty.

Defense Counsel: But guilty of what? The judge hasn't yet read you the law or the elements of the crime with which he is charged. Why do you believe he must be guilty?

Potential Juror #7: I just do. I know a lot of police. They're good people.

Defense Counsel: Thank you very much for responding so honestly. . . . *Your Honor, based on this juror's candor, I move that he be dismissed from the jury pool. . . .*[2]

But even when a prospective juror admits that he presumes the defendant guilty, it is still very difficult to remove that person from consideration. The reason is that judges have developed several ways to "rehabilitate" these would-be jurors to keep them in the jury pool and, in many cases, get them on the defendant's jury. The rehabilitation of our hypothetical "Potential Juror #7" goes like this:

Judge: . . . I am going to ask you some questions. Now, the law says that every person accused of a crime is innocent until proven guilty. Do you understand that?

Potential Juror #7: Yes.

Judge: And this defendant is only accused, and not yet convicted. Do you agree?

Potential Juror #7: Yes.

Judge: Therefore, he is presumed innocent, and you must view him that way unless the evidence proves otherwise, all right?

Potential Juror #7: If you say so.

Judge: . . . It's not what *I* say. Well, it is what I say, but it also has to be what you believe. Now, do you understand and believe that?

Potential Juror #7: Yes, Judge. I'm sorry.

Judge: . . . Don't be sorry. I want to know if *you* agree with what I said about the guilt or innocence of the defendant, and I want to know about your ability to presume him innocent. Now, do you agree with that, and can you do that?

Potential Juror #7: Um, yes. . . .

Judge: This juror is satisfactory and I will not strike him. . . .[3]

Similarly, in Avery's Halbach case, there was actual evidence of juror bias and judicial rehabilitation during the *voir dire* process. One potential juror, for example, not only stated in the juror questionnaire that Avery was probably guilty, but had also discussed the case with prosecutor Ken Kratz at a social event before the trial, where she also told *him* that Avery was probably guilty. The *voir dire* of this witness was recorded and transcribed, and went as follows:

Dean Strang: And you think you probably made a comment to Mr. Kratz that this guy [Steven Avery] was probably guilty?

Would-be Juror: I probably did, yes.

Dean Strang: That was certainly an opinion you held at the time?

Would-be Juror: Yes.[4]

Wisconsin law states that any prospective juror who "has expressed or formed any opinion" in the case "shall be excused."[5] And this prospective juror not only formed an opinion that Avery was probably guilty, but also expressed it—*twice*. She said so in response to the juror questionnaire, and she also said so to Avery's prosecutor Ken Kratz at a social event. Therefore, Dean Strang argued, because she "comes in thinking him probably guilty, rather than presumably innocent," she should be excused and should not serve on the jury.[6]

Even though dismissal of the juror would have been reasonable—and seemingly required—under Wisconsin's law, the judge instead decided to rehabilitate her. And this juror offered much less resistance than the hypothetical "Potential Juror #7" used in the earlier example. The judge's exchange with Avery's would-be juror went like this:

Judge: . . . In answer to a couple of questions on the question-naire you indicated, I believe, as I read your answers, that based on the news reports that you had heard, you thought that [Steven Avery] was probably guilty—

Would-be Juror: Yes.

Judge: —is that correct?

Would-be Juror: Yes, your Honor. . . .

Judge: So you understand that at trial, the defendant starts off with a clean slate and, in fact, that you couldn't find him guilty unless you concluded the State proved it, beyond a reasonable doubt.

Would-be Juror: Yes, mm-hmm.

Judge: So you believe you could set aside the opinion—The opinion that you had is just based on what you have heard, but you would not let that affect your judgment as a juror?

Would-be Juror: That's correct. . . .[7]

Judge: . . . [S]he felt based on those reports the defendant was probably guilty, but she also indicated she could set aside that belief if selected as a juror in this case. . . . And I'm satisfied, based on all her answers, that she is neither subjectively or [sic] objectively biased. Therefore, *the Court is going to deny the request to excuse her for cause.*[8]

This all-too-common presumption of guilt in criminal cases is probably based, at least in part, on our inexplicable trust in government—a phenomenon that was on full display in *Making a Murderer*. Even though the Manitowoc sheriff and prosecutor had wrongly arrested, convicted, and imprisoned Avery once before—while at the same time allowing Gregory Allen to remain free and victimize more women—many citizens of Manitowoc County, including this would-be juror, still blindly trusted that their government agents "got the right guy." And because of this, they presumed Avery's guilt in the Halbach case long before the first piece of evidence was presented in court.

The presumption of guilt runs wide and deep, and is not likely to be overcome by the judge's simple instruction—an instruction buried among dozens of other instructions, no less—that "[t]he law presumes every person charged with the commission of an offense to be innocent."[9] Nor is it likely to be overcome by the judge's simple rehabilitation practice where he asks leading questions that clearly indicate how he wants the juror to answer. More specifically, returning to Avery's would-be juror, there are at least two problems with the judge's rehabilitation efforts.

First, the judge's leading question was really just a multipart statement. He said, "So you believe you could set aside the opinion—The opinion that you had is just based on what you have heard, but you would not let that affect your judgment as a juror?" And the would-be juror agreed, "That's correct."[10] But *what* was correct? That she based her opinion "on what [she] had heard"? That she "could set aside the opinion"? Or that, even if she could not set it aside, she "would not let that affect [her] judgment as a juror"? The judge was in such a rush to rehabilitate the would-be juror that his compound, leading question wasn't even clear—other than he clearly wanted her to agree with him.

And second, even putting aside the linguistics problem, which is the more likely explanation for why Avery's would-be juror agreed with the judge: (1) she *really* changed her long-held belief, and all of the sudden presumed Avery to be innocent; or (2) she was merely attempting to satisfy an authority figure by telling the judge what he obviously wanted to hear? The second explanation seems more likely.

Looking at Avery's Halbach jury, no one can seriously assert that every juror started with a presumption of innocence, maintained that presumption throughout the multi-week trial, and then entered jury deliberations continuing to presume his innocence while beginning to evaluate the state's evidence. In fact, a post-conviction motion reveals the opposite: several jurors were not willing to presume innocence or to critically evaluate the state's case. One juror, "at the outset of deliberations," even confidently declared that "he's fucking guilty."[11]

This presumption of guilt is deeply ingrained in many people, is therefore unavoidable in criminal trials, and is not easily reversed. Given this reality, the manner in which the trial court instructs the jury on the state's burden of proof is incredibly important.

THE TWO BURDENS OF PROOF

Many people are not comfortable with the concept of probability; rather, they like to view things in black-and-white terms. Either something happened, or it didn't. Further, many people are overconfident in their ability to divine the truth of what actually happened in any given situation.

But if jurors are to do their jobs in accordance with their oath, they must be a bit more sophisticated in their thinking; they must evaluate the big picture in terms of probability. For example, in a civil case involving a breach-of-contract lawsuit, the plaintiff carries the burden of proof and, in order to prevail at trial, must prove his, her, or its case—yes, "its"; corporations are frequent-flyer plaintiffs in the American court system—by the preponderance of the evidence. Some people like to think of the phrase "preponderance of the evidence" as meaning more likely than not, or, in numerical terms, 50.1 percent of the quantum of evidence.

In criminal cases, however, the burden of proof is much higher: the state, in order to prevail, must prove its case "beyond a reasonable doubt."[12] This higher burden of proof is justified for two reasons. First, with regard to individual defendants, this burden is needed to protect us "from dubious and unjust convictions, with resulting forfeitures of life, liberty and property."[13] And second, with regard to society more generally, this burden "is indispensable to command the respect and confidence of the community in applications of the criminal law."[14] In light of these concerns, therefore, "[i]t is critical that the moral force of the criminal law not be diluted" by a lower burden of proof.[15]

Despite the constitutional importance of the burden of proof, the US Supreme Court surprisingly does not require state trial courts to use any specific language in their jury instructions.[16] As a result, courts across the country have struggled with how to define the phrase "reasonable doubt" for juries. One of the best, simplest, and clearest ways to explain the concept to a criminal jury is to describe it in relative terms: "In civil cases, it is only necessary to prove that a fact is more likely true than not or that its truth is highly probable. *In criminal cases such as this, the State's proof must be more powerful than that. It must be beyond a reasonable doubt.*"[17]

Unfortunately for Avery and Dassey, Wisconsin courts do not define reasonable doubt this way. Rather, Wisconsin courts do two very troubling things. First, they define reasonable doubt, in part, as follows: "It means such a doubt as would cause a person of ordinary prudence to pause or hesitate when called upon to act in the most important affairs of life."[18] This analogy may, at first glance, seem reasonable. However, there are many criticisms of this definition, including that "decisions we make in the most important affairs of our lives—choosing a spouse, a job, a place to live, and the like—generally involve a very heavy element of uncertainty and risk-taking. They are wholly *unlike* the decisions jurors ought to make in criminal cases."[19]

But second, there is a much bigger problem. After defining reasonable doubt, Wisconsin courts strangely conclude their jury instruction by telling the jury to brush aside any such doubts. More specifically, Wisconsin's standard jury instruction concludes, "[Y]ou are *not* to search for doubt. You are to search *for the truth*."[20]

THE TROUBLE WITH TRUTH

The problem with instructing the jury not to examine the state's evidence for doubt, but instead "to search for the truth" of what they think really happened, is that it lowers the burden of proof below the constitutionally guaranteed reasonable doubt standard. That is, it sends the burden of proof careening back to the more likely than not standard used in civil cases. As one federal court observed, "seeking the truth suggests determining whose version of events is more likely true, the government's or the defendant's, and thereby intimates a *preponderance of the evidence* standard."[21]

In other words, if a jury feels the government's version of events is only *slightly* more likely than the defendant's—in numeric terms, 50.1 percent of the quantum of evidence—it would follow that, in a search for the truth, the jury would be obligated to convict. But this, of course, would violate our constitutional right to remain free of conviction unless the state proves its case beyond a reasonable doubt.

Defense lawyers in Wisconsin have frequently objected to this bizarre, burden-lowering jury instruction,[22] to which prosecutors and judges have developed two standard responses.

First, the government contends that the instruction to disregard doubt in favor of a search for the truth is appropriate because trials *are* searches for the truth.[23] This claim may at first appear to be merely simplistic or naïve; however, it is actually disingenuous. In reality, Wisconsin courts have developed numerous trial rules that actually exclude defendants' evidence of innocence, thereby suppressing the truth rather than revealing it. We saw an example in chapter 5, where Wisconsin's Denny rule prevented Avery from arguing that a third party, Gregory Allen, attacked Penny Beerntsen. Similarly, this same rule prevented Jerry Buting and Dean Strang from presenting evidence that a specific third party, other than Avery and Dassey, murdered Halbach. When courts ensure that such evidence is hidden from the jury, they are doing many things, but promoting a search for the truth is not one of them.

But even if seeking the truth was the real goal of a jury trial, such truth-related language has no part in a burden of proof jury instruction. As a Washington State appellate court realized, "truth is not the jury's job."[24] Rather, "The question for any jury is whether the burden of proof has been carried by the party who bears it. In a criminal case . . . [t]he jury cannot discern whether that has occurred without examining the evidence for reasonable doubt."[25]

The second response developed by the government is that, even if truth-seeking is not the primary goal of the jury trial system, the instruction "to search for the truth" probably does not harm defendants in any way. The reason, prosecutors and courts contend, is that reasonable doubt is adequately defined elsewhere within Wisconsin's standard jury instruction; therefore, the argument goes, the jury will simply disregard the instruction's truth-related language and will instead follow the instruction's reasonable doubt mandate.[26]

PUTTING IT TO THE TEST

Lawrence White and I decided to test whether Wisconsin's truth-related language lowers the burden of proof or, as the government contends, does not have any effect on juror decision making.[27] To test our hypothesis, we recruited 298 participants to serve as mock jurors in a controlled study. Each juror then read the identical case summary of a hypothetical criminal trial. The case summary included the elements of the charged crime, a summary of the witness testimony, and the closing arguments of the lawyers. Jurors were then randomly assigned to one of three groups, with each group receiving a different jury instruction on the state's burden of proof.

Group A received a very short burden of proof instruction, and was simply told "to search for the truth"; this group convicted at a rate of 29.6 percent.[28] Group B received a legally proper reasonable doubt instruction that concluded with the mandate to "give the defendant the benefit of every reasonable doubt"; this group convicted at a rate of only 16 percent.[29] Finally, Group C received Wisconsin's standard jury instruction, which defines reasonable doubt but then concludes by instructing jurors "not to search for doubt," but instead "to search for the truth." This group's conviction rate jumped back up to 29 percent.[30]

Group C—the group that received Wisconsin's standard jury instruction—convicted at a rate nearly double that of the group that received a legally proper reasonable doubt instruction, and was statistically identical to the group that received no reasonable doubt instruction whatsoever.

Due to the large sample size of our study and the large gap in conviction rates, these findings were statistically significant.[31] This is strong empirical evidence that Wisconsin's jury instruction—instructing jurors to disregard doubt in favor of an unrealistic and misplaced search for the truth—not only lowers, but actually eviscerates, the state's burden of proof in criminal cases. These findings also empirically prove what the prosecutors in the Avery and Dassey trials probably already knew: it was easier to convict Avery and Dassey (and every other Wisconsin criminal defendant) when the judge instructs the jury not to evaluate the state's evidence for reasonable doubt, but instead to search for the truth of what they think really happened.

AVERY'S JURIES AND THE BURDEN OF PROOF

It is interesting to think of Wisconsin's burden-lowering jury instruction in the context of Avery's trial for the Beerntsen rape. The jurors in that case were instructed "to search for the truth."[32] And when they heard Beerntsen's powerful and compelling testimony that Avery had brutally attacked her, they no doubt equated her passion and emotion with "the truth," and found Avery guilty. After all, she testified that she was positive Avery was the attacker, and she had no reason to (intentionally) falsely accuse him.

But had the jurors been instructed, as the Constitution requires, simply to search the state's evidence for "reasonable doubt,"[33] the jury's focus may have shifted to Avery's denial, the sixteen alibi witnesses who placed him far away from the crime scene, and the complete absence of any physical evidence linking him to the crime. When viewed in this light, it is quite possible that Wisconsin's standard jury instruction was at least partially responsible for Avery's wrongful conviction—and the eighteen years he spent in prison for a crime he did not commit.

Even worse, in the Halbach murder trial, Wisconsin's burden-lowering jury instruction may have cost Avery his freedom for the rest of his life. We know from *Making a Murderer* that the initial poll of jurors included seven that believed Avery was *not* guilty, yet in the end they could not carry the day. Instead, the other jurors were more passionate, believed they knew the truth, and were able to win in the end. A post-conviction motion takes us inside the jury room and reveals the completely different mindsets of two of the jurors, Juror N and Juror G:

> Juror N was one of the 12 jurors to whom the case was submitted. He had never before served on a jury. The defense perceived him as a favorable juror or at least someone who would come to his own view of the case. Juror N entered deliberations planning to make a

decision after an examination of all of the evidence. Accordingly, in a preliminary vote taken during the first day of deliberations, Juror N voted not guilty. He became frustrated, however, by comments from three jurors that suggested an unwillingness to look at all the evidence. In particular, Juror N was disturbed by Juror G's comment, made at the outset of deliberations, that "he's fucking guilty." Due to the jurors' comments and the attitude those comments seemed to convey, Juror N left deliberations that day feeling angry, hopeless and frustrated. Juror N's mood worsened during dinner. . . . In a sarcastic tone, Juror G [said to Juror N], "If you can't handle it, why don't you tell them and just leave." Given Juror G's demeanor and tone of voice and his comment during deliberations, Juror N felt verbally threatened and upset.[34]

Juror N—who left the jury and was replaced by an alternate juror—took his duty seriously: he wanted to examine the evidence to see if it amounted to proof beyond a reasonable doubt. Until that happened, he presumed Steven Avery's innocence and voted not guilty in the initial poll. Juror G, on the other hand, had his mind made up, had presumed Avery's guilt, and was unwilling to change that view.

But while Juror N was carrying out his constitutionally mandated duty, Wisconsin's jury instruction on the burden of proof was enabling other jurors (like Juror G) to follow their emotions. That is, although Wisconsin's instruction discusses the concept of reasonable doubt, its conclusion sends a clear message to jurors who have already presumed guilt: "[Y]ou are *not* to search for doubt. You are to search for the *truth*."[35]

The all-too-common presumption of guilt, combined with Wisconsin's "search for the truth" jury instruction, is a dangerous cocktail. As Avery's defense lawyer Dean Strang explained, judges, prosecutors, and many jurors proceed with an unwarranted level of certitude, thinking they can *know* things even without evidence. And, unfortunately, Wisconsin's jury instruction only exacerbates, rather than mitigates, that serious problem.

Chapter 8

INSUFFICIENT EVIDENCE

"Where is the blood?"

—Dean Strang

T he last chapter demonstrated that criminal juries in Wisconsin are convicting defendants on a mere "preponderance of the evidence" standard, rather than a "beyond a reasonable doubt" standard. And, worse yet, once a jury convicts a defendant, that conviction is incredibly difficult to overturn—even when the jury's verdict is completely irrational. For example, in the Halbach case, the jurors found Avery *not* guilty of burning the corpse, but *guilty* of the underlying murder—an irrational split verdict that not even Ken Kratz could have hoped for (but gladly accepted).

More specifically, when a defendant wants a new trial, he "bears a heavy burden in attempting to set aside a jury's verdict on the grounds of *insufficient evidence*. Evidence is insufficient to sustain a conviction only if the evidence, when viewed most favorably to the State, is so insufficient in probative value and force that it can be said as a matter of law that no trier of fact, acting reasonably," could have convicted the defendant.[1]

How does Avery's Teresa Halbach murder case fit into this framework? Could a jury, "acting reasonably," have found him guilty under any standard, let alone beyond a reasonable doubt? Before analyzing the evidence, let's briefly recap the state's and the defense team's arguments as presented in *Making a Murderer*.

THEORIES OF THE CASE

The prosecutor argued that Avery killed Halbach either in his trailer or his garage. (The bloody rape and torture and throat slashing allegedly occurred in the trailer; the shooting allegedly occurred in the garage.) The prosecutor then contended that, after killing her, Avery dragged her a few feet to a burn pit—less than a stone's throw from his bedroom window—where he incinerated her body. He then moved her car, accidentally leaving his blood inside of it, and kept her car key in his bedroom.

The defense team, on the other hand, argued that someone other than Avery killed Halbach and burned her remains. (Wisconsin's Denny rule, however, prevented them from telling the jury who, specifically, they believed committed the crimes.) The murderer knew that the Manitowoc Sheriff's Department hated Avery, believed he was a violent criminal, and would immediately suspect him of killing Halbach. So the murderer put Halbach's car and her physical remains on the Avery property. Finally, the Manitowoc sheriffs—firmly convinced of Avery's guilt from the get-go—provided the finishing touches by planting some additional evidence. In the cops' minds, they were simply framing a guilty man.[2]

But given these theories of the case, how do we decide whether the "probative value and force" of the evidence was enough for a jury, "acting reasonably," to convict Avery of murdering Halbach? The analysis of Avery's case begs for a version of the "unluckiest defendant" argument.

THE UNLUCKIEST DEFENDANT IN THE WORLD

When prosecutors make their closing arguments to juries, they commonly summarize the facts of the case by fitting them into the unluckiest defendant framework. They will argue that, if the defendant is truly innocent as he contends, then he must be the unluckiest person in the world. Here's an example of a prosecutor's unluckiest defendant argument in the context of a hypothetical burglary case:

Mr. Defendant claims he is innocent of this burglary. Well, let's see. His shoe prints are *inside* of the victim's house. The neighbor testified that he saw him coming *out* of the victim's house. And finally, the police caught him with the stolen property in *his* house. For all of these things to happen to an innocent man, this defendant must be the unluckiest person in the world! Ask yourselves, ladies and gentlemen, which is more likely? That someone with shoes just like his, who looks just like him, decided to burglarize the victim's house, and then generously give him the stolen property? Or is it more likely that *this* defendant is the one who burglarized the victim's house? In other words, is the man who sits before you the unluckiest defendant in the world? Or is he guilty of the crime? Of course he's guilty, ladies and gentlemen of the jury.

This argument harnesses the appeal of probabilities. The prosecutor is arguing that, in order to believe the defendant is innocent, you must believe that an incredibly long string of events occurred. Each of the events, individually, would be highly unlikely. But to have them all occur together is nearly impossible. Had all of this really happened, this defendant would have to be the unluckiest defendant in the world. And by comparison, the prosecutor's second option— that the defendant is guilty—looks much more attractive. (Much like Mark Wiegert and Tom Fassbender did when interrogating Brendan Dassey, prosecutors will construct an "option number two.")

Using some variations on this common, prosecutorial theme is the perfect way to analyze the evidence in Avery's case.

THE DUMBEST DEFENDANT IN THE WORLD

Ken Kratz claimed that, after the murder, Steven Avery had to get rid of Halbach's car. Avery lives on a forty-acre junkyard with several thousand cars on it. There is even a car crusher on the property. So how did he decide to get rid of the most important piece of evidence against him? Did he crush the car in the car crusher? No. Did he at least park it in the middle of the property among the several thousand other cars so it would blend in and never be discovered? No.

According to Kratz, Avery is the dumbest defendant in the world. He decided to drive the car to the far edge of his forty-acre property where it would be most visible to the public. He then decided to drive it up onto a ridge, where it would be even easier to spot. He even made it stand out like a sore thumb by leaning something against it and putting some tree branches on top of it—all the while leaving the car itself easy to see and identify. That's right: Avery was so dumb that he parked the biggest piece of evidence against him—both literally and figuratively—where it would most likely be discovered. In fact, Halbach's car was so easily spotted that an amateur searcher—a person who had never before been on the forty-acre, car-filled property—found the car and cracked the case within thirty-five minutes of setting foot on Avery's property. (Much like Jerry Buting, I, too, reject the witness's divine intervention theory for explaining how she found the car so quickly.)

Now, what is more likely? That Avery was the absolute dumbest defendant in the world and went to great effort to put the car in the one place where it would definitely be discovered? Or is it more likely that the real murderer killed Halbach at another location, put her body in her car (thus explaining why her blood was found inside), drove her car to the edge of the Avery property, and parked it on a ridge where someone was sure to see it and connect Avery to the crime?

Without question, the frame job is the far more likely scenario. But if you still believe the prosecutor and think that Avery is the dumbest defendant in the world, just wait a minute. The prosecutor also argues that Avery is the smartest guy you'd ever meet.

THE SMARTEST DEFENDANT IN THE WORLD

Ken Kratz sometimes claimed that Avery killed Halbach in his trailer. Like a bad novelist, he painted a way-too-detailed picture for the media, creepily describing Avery as "partially dressed, full of sweat," and referring to him as Dassey's "sweaty, forty-three-year-old uncle."[3] With tremendous confidence, he went on to describe Avery's incredibly bloody stabbing, throat slashing, and murder of Halbach while she was tied to his bed, spewing blood all over the place.

Other times, however, Kratz abandoned this detail-rich story and even changed the location of the murder, simply saying that Avery shot Halbach in the head, at close range, in his garage.

Regardless of the location, the burning question is this: where is Halbach's blood? The state's explanation is that Avery is a mad genius and a highly skilled forensic scientist. The same man who was dumb enough to park Halbach's car up on a ridge on the very edge of his property—the one place where it was sure to be discovered—was smart and skilled enough to eliminate Halbach's blood and all traces of her DNA from the trailer and garage.

Of course, this is not possible. First, no person would simultaneously be that stupid and that brilliant. But second, the sheriffs and other government agents didn't just look for blood with the naked eye. They searched Avery's trailer at least six times, and at one point had several cops on hands and knees, combing the floor to collect samples of invisible forensic evidence. No blood or DNA was ever found, despite the allegation that Avery repeatedly stabbed and slashed her, and then carried her blood-drenched body out of the trailer. And there was no evidence that the residence had been cleaned; in fact, Avery's own DNA was all over it, as would be expected.

But even the state wasn't convinced of its own theory, so it also searched Avery's garage for days. Government agents examined every single item in that cluttered mess—items that would have contained Halbach's blood spatter from close-range shots to the head. They even broke up the cement floor to look for the blood that, had Halbach actually been killed there, would have inevitably found its way into the cracks and crevices. In the end, their search of the garage was as fruitless as their search of the trailer.

Not a single piece of evidence in or from the trailer, or in or from the garage, put Halbach inside either location, save for one bullet that actually tested inconclusive for her DNA (see chapter 4 for more details on that). Therefore, the state's position was that the same Steven Avery who failed to crush Halbach's car—or at least hide it among the thousands of other cars on his forty-acre property—was brilliant enough to sanitize the trailer and garage of all of her blood and DNA, while at the same time leaving his own DNA intact. He must be the smartest defendant in the world.

If you believe the prosecutor that Avery's pure brilliance and forensic skill allowed him to eliminate all of the blood and DNA evidence, just hold on. The prosecutor changed his mind again: Avery is the dumbest defendant in the world after all.

THE DUMBEST DEFENDANT IN THE WORLD (AGAIN)

Another piece of evidence in the case was the pile of Halbach's bone fragments. Nearly all of her bones were found very close to Avery's trailer and garage, in the burn pit. However, and very importantly, two human bone fragments were found far, far away in the quarry.

According to Ken Kratz, Avery decided to incinerate Halbach's body right outside his trailer and garage, and in doing so overlooked two important things. First, this huge fire would be easily seen by outsiders. And second, when the bone fragments were eventually discovered, their physical location—right next to Avery's home and garage—would mean only one thing: Avery did it.

What is more likely? That Avery is the dumbest defendant in the world and incinerated the corpse in plain view of others—leaving the evidence right next to his own house and garage, no less—and then took only two small bone fragments and transported them far away to the quarry for no apparent reason? Or is it more likely that the real murderer incinerated the body at the quarry, transported the remains to the burn pit right outside Avery's trailer, and accidentally left two small bone fragments behind?

Of course, once again, the frame job is more likely. But if you're confused by the prosecutor's argument, and can't decide whether Avery is an idiot or a genius or both, let's take a closer look at some of the other evidence and arguments.

WHAT'S MY MOTIVATION?

We know from chapter 5 that Wisconsin law does not allow a defendant to blame a specific third party for the crime unless he can demonstrate, among other things, the third party's motive. And we also learned there is a double standard: the prosecutor does not have to prove the defendant's motive in order to convict him. But even though the prosecutor isn't required to prove the defendant's motive, he can still try to if he wants. And similarly, the defendant's *lack* of motive can be used at trial as well.

What motive did Steven Avery possibly have for wanting Halbach dead? Avery had been free for about two years after he was exonerated in the Beerntsen rape case. Halbach had been to his junkyard to photograph cars numerous times, and everything was uneventful—so uneventful, in fact, that she returned yet again to photograph another car. And Avery's life was great and getting better. The legislature was passing a law to give him $450,000 for his wrongful incarceration, he had a multimillion-dollar lawsuit pending against the Manitowoc Sheriff's Department, and he was a celebrity of sorts in the legal and political communities. He simply had no motive—either against Halbach or in general—to commit murder.

But if Avery was really innocent, that would mean that the Manitowoc sheriffs did something to frame him. Contrary to Ken Kratz's disingenuous closing argument—see chapter 13 for more on that—the defense never suggested that the sheriffs *killed* Halbach. Rather, the defense argued that an unknown third party killed her, and the sheriffs were so eager to pin the crime on Avery—just as they had been in the Beerntsen case—that they planted evidence to ensure his conviction. In particular, they would have planted Avery's blood in Halbach's car and her car key in his bedroom.

But what would be the sheriffs' motive for wanting Avery convicted? *Making a Murderer* presented evidence that the sheriffs absolutely despised Avery even before his first conviction. The documentary made a compelling case that a road rage incident between Avery and the wife of a sheriff's deputy led the sheriffs to ignore the real perpetrator, and focus solely on Avery, in the Beerntsen case. This, in turn, led to his wrongful conviction and eventual release (eighteen years later) when DNA evidence proved that Gregory Allen was the real perpetrator.

Words simply cannot convey how devastating this series of events was for the Manitowoc Sheriff's Department. Because of their tunnel vision, not only was Avery wrongfully incarcerated, but Gregory Allen remained free and victimized more women in the community. This is a heavy cross to bear. On top of that, the sheriff's department was being sued civilly, key employees had to testify under oath in depositions, and the department was potentially on the hook for many millions of dollars.

Not surprisingly, the sheriffs reacted to this tremendous burden by going into denial mode. At least two high-ranking officials within the department—Ken Petersen and Gene Kusche—questioned Avery's DNA exoneration and maintained that Avery might still, after all, be guilty of the Beerntsen rape. They also believed, beyond any doubt, that he was guilty of the Halbach murder. And if their belief was true, it would solve a lot of the department's problems.

First, as a practical matter, if Avery murdered Halbach it would be the death blow to his civil lawsuit against the sheriff's department. Second, murdering Halbach would get many people thinking that, despite his earlier DNA exoneration, maybe the sheriffs were right: Avery might have been Beerntsen's attacker after all. And third, at the very least, everyone would be thinking what one politician, Mark Gundrum, said aloud: "And then ya start thinkin' ta yourself, boy, maybe it was good he was in all that time, as unjust as it was. If he did this [the Halbach murder], what might he have done during that time?"[4]

According to the documentary, many employees of the Manitowoc Sheriff's Department therefore had a motive to pin the Halbach murder on Avery. Even those in charge of the Halbach investigation knew this, and, during a press conference, acknowledged the conflict—or at least the appearance of a conflict—and promised that the Manitowoc sheriffs would play only a very limited, supporting role in the investigation. (This promise, however, went unfulfilled.)

And if any doubts about the Manitowoc sheriffs still lingered, those were soon put to rest. The documentary showed television footage of Ken Petersen, the top dog in the department, talking about Avery. In an incredibly eerie, unsettling interview, he publicly discussed both hypothetically framing and hypothetically killing Steven Avery. Killing Avery, he insisted, would have been easier, and the sheriffs would have preferred that option to framing him; therefore, his argument continued, the sheriffs were *not* guilty of framing him—a compelling and confidence-inspiring statement from a public official.

But even if the sheriffs had a theoretical motive to frame Avery, is there any evidence that they actually did so? After all, such a frame job would require a vast conspiracy within the department, and, quite obviously, many of them could not keep a simple story straight from one court hearing to the next. Surely, such an elaborate frame job was beyond their limited capabilities, wasn't it?

THE MISSING LENK

Whenever a defendant alleges some sort of government or police wrongdoing, prosecutors like to portray the defendant as a crackpot conspiracy theorist. Prosecutors usually argue that such elaborate, conspiratorial schemes would simply be too difficult to pull off.

But this mischaracterizes Avery's defense team's argument. Avery's lawyers made clear that no conspiracy was required to put Avery's blood in Halbach's car and to put Halbach's car key in Avery's bedroom. Rather, as Jerry Buting stated, "One guy's name just kept coming up, over and over and over, every place we looked, at critical moments. And that was Lieutenant James Lenk."[5]

Lenk had signed the transmittal documents for the physical evidence in Avery's first case, meaning that he was aware the sheriffs still possessed a vial of Avery's blood. (The seal on the box was also broken, and the top of the vial was punctured, leaving a needle-sized hole from which blood may have been extracted.)[6] Lenk also had access to Halbach's car; in fact, he signed the log that tracked who came near the car and the crime scene—more on that in a moment. Finally, even though the Manitowoc Sheriff's Department was barred from participating in the investigation due to its conflict of interest, Lenk was the one who found Halbach's car key—allegedly in plain view on Avery's bedroom floor—but not until the cops' *sixth* search of his trailer.

The point, of course, is that for purposes of evaluating the evidence for reasonable doubt, no vast conspiracy was needed. Instead, it all came down to just one person. And there is little doubt that this one person, Lenk, had the *opportunity* to plant the blood and the key (and even the so-called magic bullet).[7] But he testified under oath that he did not. This leads to the question, is he a believable witness? One way to determine that is to see whether he was being consistent in other parts of his testimony—and this is where the sign-in log and Halbach's car come into play.

Once Halbach's car was identified and located on Avery's property, law enforcement secured the scene and required everyone coming near that area to sign a log. And Lenk did, in fact, sign the log. But the problem is that he signed *out*, but did not sign *in*. The defense wanted to draw the conclusion that Lenk did not sign in because he was evading detection so he could plant the blood evidence. And Lenk's testimony certainly helped Avery's cause.

Lenk testified at trial that he arrived at the scene around 2:00 p.m., or possibly 2:05 p.m., which could have been before the other law enforcement officers initiated the log and sign-in procedure. This, of course, would explain why he signed out, but not in. But the problem for Lenk is that he had previously testified under oath, in another hearing in the case, that he had arrived at the scene around 6:30 p.m. or 7:00 p.m.—which would have been well after the log and sign-in procedure had been instituted. When pressed, Lenk admitted that he changed his testimony, and further admitted that if he had arrived there at 7:00 p.m., as he had previously testified, it would be very difficult to explain why he hadn't signed in on the log. Lenk's two versions of when he arrived were also contradicted by his own timesheets where he recorded what he did, and how long it took him to do it, for the entire day.[8]

The defense effectively argued that this was not a fifteen-minute discrepancy, or even a two-hour discrepancy. Rather, it was a *five-hour* discrepancy. But worse yet for Lenk and the state, even aside from the five-hour gap, this is not likely to be a point of mere forgetfulness. As the defense also pointed out, during the month of November in the state of Wisconsin, the difference between 2:00 p.m. and 7:00 p.m. is the difference between broad daylight and pitch black. These two points in time are simply not easily confused, particularly for a trained law enforcement officer investigating an incredibly serious and highly unusual crime—one he likely would not forget or confuse with his run-of-the-mill casework.

So, in short, for purposes of a reasonable doubt analysis, a vast conspiracy was not needed to frame Steven Avery. Instead, the defense argued that two people, and possibly only one person, could have pulled it off. One person knew about, and had access to, Avery's vial of blood from the previous case; that same person had access to Halbach's car, did not sign in on the log, and then couldn't testify consistently about what time he arrived at the scene; that same person also happened to find Halbach's car key, on the government's sixth search of a small room, that everyone else happened to overlook in the first five searches; that same person was also on the property when the so-called magic bullet was discovered; and, finally, that same person should never have been involved in the investigation because of his earlier deposition and his employer's conflict of interest as a defendant in Avery's civil suit.

To borrow the lingo from the three-party Denny test discussed in chapter 5, the defense made a strong argument that there was not just motive and opportunity, but also evidence of a frame job.[9] Or, to put it in Dean Strang's words, "I've sat in many a federal courtroom and heard federal prosecutors prove a conspiracy on less than we've heard already. . . ."[10]

"PROBATIVE VALUE AND FORCE"

Returning, then, to our original question, did the state's case have enough "probative value and force" for a jury, "acting reasonably," to convict Avery?

To summarize, Halbach's car was on Avery's property, but, given its location, it was more likely put there by a person trying to frame Avery than by Avery himself. Halbach's bone fragments were found on Avery's property, but the circumstances demonstrated that she was incinerated elsewhere, and her remains were transported *to* the property. The physical evidence overwhelmingly (if not conclusively) demonstrated that Halbach never set foot in either Avery's trailer or garage—the two alleged murder locations. Because the Manitowoc Sheriff's Department had motives to pin the crime on Avery, their employees were barred from participating in the investigation. Yet, it was a Manitowoc Sheriff's Department employee who found Halbach's car key, sitting in plain view on the floor of Avery's bedroom—something every other law enforcement officer supposedly missed during their first five searches of the room. (Also, even though she possessed the key for six years, and Avery allegedly possessed it only for a few days, the key strangely contained only Avery's DNA and not Halbach's.)

This seems to add up to reasonable doubt, rather than guilt. And this may explain why seven jurors initially voted that Avery was not the perpetrator. It may also explain why, in the end, the jurors never agreed. Rather, they irrationally split the verdict after a lengthy deliberation, nonsensically finding Avery guilty of murder but not guilty of mutilating a corpse.

But is the evidence so weak that the state appellate court would reverse the conviction? Not even close. Earlier chapters explained how the courts abuse the word "reasonable," and how that word spells certain doom for the defendant. And under this sufficiency of the evidence test, as long as the jury is "acting reasonably"—there is that dreaded word again—the conviction will stand.

In fact, in Avery's case, given the appellate court's incredibly generous interpretation of what is reasonable, even a single piece of evidence standing alone would probably have been sufficient to uphold the conviction. That is, just the car, or just the physical remains, or just the key—no matter where the item was located or by whom it was found—would probably be enough to sustain the jury's verdict. But when all three pieces of evidence are combined, as they were in Avery's case, the court simply has to decide: Is this the unluckiest defendant in the world? Or is this defendant guilty? Just like the jury, the state appellate judges will select option number two every time—the defendant is guilty, and the conviction will stand.

Chapter 9

POSTMORTEM ON PRELIMINARY HEARINGS

"It is my belief, having attended the preliminary hearing, that there is a tremendous opportunity to present a real and substantial defense."

—Walter Kelly

Much of the focus of *Making a Murderer* was on Steven Avery's trial in the Teresa Halbach case. The jury trial, after all, is where the action happens. It's where the drama unfolds. It's where witnesses are caught in their lies, where so-called experts are tripped up and made to look like amateurs, and where the lawyers make their dramatic closing arguments. But long before the trial, and shortly after the state first filed its criminal complaint, Avery had a hearing called the preliminary examination, or preliminary hearing. In many ways, this hearing shaped the future of his case and helped seal his fate.

PRELIMINARY HEARING BASICS

Often confused with the initial appearance or the arraignment, the preliminary hearing is actually an evidentiary hearing where the state calls witnesses and sometimes presents other evidence.[1] A judge or court commissioner presides over the hearing, but a jury is not involved. After the hearing, the judge decides whether the state's case is strong enough to continue to the next stage of the criminal process. If it is, the judge will bind the defendant over for further proceedings. If it is not, the judge must dismiss the case.

Avery's civil rights lawyer, Walter Kelly, was being perfectly reasonable when he uttered the above quote about preliminary hearings. Minimal research even reveals a wealth of grandiose court language to support his belief. For example, the Supreme Court of Wisconsin has held that the preliminary hearing was designed

> to prevent hasty, malicious, improvident and oppressive prosecutions, to protect the person charged from open and public accusations of crime, to avoid both for the defendant and the public the expense of a public trial, and to save the defendant from the humiliation and anxiety involved in public prosecution, and to discover whether or not there are substantial grounds upon which a prosecution may be based.[2]

These promises, however, turn out to be empty. Not only does the preliminary hearing fail to protect against "hasty, malicious, improvident and oppressive prosecutions," but it has morphed into a dangerous prosecutorial weapon. In Avery's case, the preliminary hearing probably played a role in his high cash bail,[3] and, as explained later in this chapter, most certainly played a central role in the state's ability to stack the charges against him. (At one time, Avery faced six criminal counts, and fighting them sapped much of the defense team's time, energy, and resources.)

But to understand the preliminary hearing, how it failed to protect Steven Avery, and how it even worked against him, we first have to take one small step back in the criminal process.

THE CRIMINAL COMPLAINT

Before a defendant in Wisconsin gets to the preliminary hearing, the state first has to charge him by filing a criminal complaint.[4] In Wisconsin, the complaint is a written document that sets forth the specific criminal statutes the defendant is alleged to have violated, along with the potential penalties associated with those charges. In

Wisconsin is open for business.
Photo by Michael Cicchini.

Avery Road, near the sign for the Avery salvage yard.
Photo by Rebecca Slye.

No trespassing.
Photo by Rebecca Slye.

The Avery property.
Photo by Rebecca Slye.

The Avery business.
Photo by Rebecca Slye.

The Avery salvage yard.
Photo by Rebecca Slye.

The Manitowoc County Sheriff's Department.
Photo by Brenda VanCuick.

Manitowoc County Courthouse.
Photo by Matthew Murray.

Brendan Dassey's juvenile detention center.
Photo by Sarvan Singh.

Manitowoc County Jail.
Photo by Matthew Murray.

At the Calumet County Sheriff's Department.
Photo by Sarvan Singh.

Calumet County Courthouse.
Photo by Sarvan Singh.

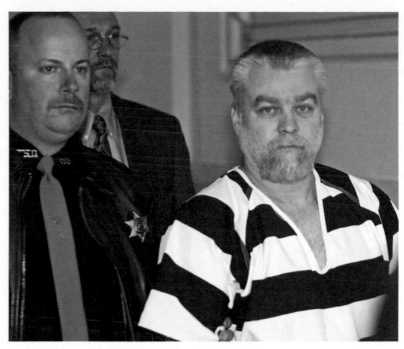

Steven Avery, right, is escorted into a Manitowoc County courtroom for his preliminary
hearing Tuesday, December 6, 2005, in Manitowoc, Wisconsin.
Photo by AP Photo/ Morry Gash.

The lawyers' conference during jury selection.
Photo by AP Photo/ Benny Sieu, Pool.

Dean Strang gets technical.
Photo by AP Photo/ Bruce Halmo, Pool.

Steven Avery at the defense table with Jerry Buting.
Photo by AP Photo/ Kirk Wagner, Pool.

Jerry Buting questions Tom Fassbender.
Photo by AP Photo/ Kirk Wagner, Pool.

Prosecutor Ken Kratz huddles with his team.
Photo by AP Photo/ Kirk Wagner, Pool.

Lt. James Lenk enters the courtroom to testify.
Photo by AP Photo/ Kirk Wagner, Pool.

Sgt. Andrew Colborn questioned by Dean Strang.
Photo by AP Photo/ Kirk Wagner, Pool.

Judge Patrick Willis holds a sidebar with Strang and Kratz.
Photo by AP Photo/ Kirk Wagner, Pool.

Brendan Dassey on his way to court.
Photo by AP Photo/ Herald Times Reporter, *Eric Young.*

Wisconsin State Capitol in Madison.
Photo by Leo Martin.

Federal courthouse in Milwaukee.
Photo by Michael Cicchini.

the Halbach case, Avery's original complaint alleged two counts: murder (more formally known as first-degree intentional homicide) and mutilating a corpse.[5]

Just as important, however, the criminal complaint also has a "probable cause" section, where it sets forth the underlying factual allegations that serve as the basis for those charges. Avery's criminal complaint read, in part, as follows:

> Complainant is informed that on November 5, 2005, officers received information from volunteer searchers that they had located a vehicle matching the description of the vehicle owned by Teresa Halbach at Avery Auto Salvage located on Avery Road in . . . Manitowoc, Wisconsin. Volunteer searchers had received verbal consent to search Avery Auto Salvage yard by Earl Avery. . . . Complainant is informed that on November 7, 2005, Deputy Dan Kucharski continued the search of the defendant's bedroom located at 12932 Avery Road . . . Manitowoc County, Wisconsin. Deputy Kucharski located a Toyota ignition key adjacent to furniture found within the bedroom of the defendant, Steven Avery. Complainant is informed that the key located in the bedroom of Steven Avery's residence was successfully used in the ignition of the Toyota Rav 4 owned by Teresa M. Halbach; the key successfully turned the ignition of the Halbach vehicle.[6]

It doesn't matter that the complaint contains multiple levels of hearsay. Notice in the above excerpt that Earl Avery spoke to "volunteer searchers," who in turn spoke to "officers," who in turn spoke to the "complainant," who then put this information into the complaint. And sometimes the source of the information isn't even clear. For example, who says that the key "successfully turned the ignition of the Halbach vehicle"? Was this something that began as mere wishful thinking—for example, "That key *probably* belongs to her car!"—and was then repeated so many times that law enforcement came to believe it? Or did someone literally put the key into the ignition and start the engine?

Further, these multiple layers of hearsay need only satisfy the legal standard of "probable cause." The probable cause test is an incredibly low bar that the state can hurdle by reciting only "minimal factual disclosures" that "need not be independently documented or delineated. . . ."[7] Also, the facts themselves do not have to establish probable cause; rather, "inferences reasonably drawn from the facts" can also be considered.[8] And the test of probable cause is to be decided not "in a hypertechnical sense, but in a minimally adequate way. . . ."[9] In short, to find probable cause in a complaint, the judge simply has to be able to answer this question: "What makes you think that the defendant committed the offense charged?"[10]

Most fourth graders would be able to draft a legally sufficient criminal complaint that satisfies the probable cause standard. But the next step in the proceeding, the preliminary hearing, is designed to test the allegations contained within the complaint. Surely this hearing, which is designed "to discover whether or not there are substantial grounds upon which a prosecution may be based," would protect Avery from any "hasty, malicious, improvident and oppressive prosecutions" by the Manitowoc County Sheriff's Department and district attorney's office.

THE PRELIMINARY HEARING AND THE BURDEN OF PROOF

For purposes of this chapter, we'll focus on one particular piece of evidence: the car key. The complaint against Avery alleged that "Deputy Dan Kucharski continued the search of the defendant's bedroom . . . [and] located a Toyota ignition key" that fit Halbach's car, which was also on Avery's property. This was an important factual allegation that was needed to establish probable cause for purposes of the compliant.[11]

But talk—particularly when it is embedded in multiple levels of hearsay—is cheap. So what happened when Kucharski took the stand and testified, under oath, at the preliminary hearing?

In *Making a Murderer*, Kucharski testified that, when searching Avery's bedroom, law enforcement moved a pair of slippers that were sitting on Avery's floor, and no key was located underneath them (or anywhere else, for that matter). But then, during their sixth search of Avery's bedroom, the key just appeared out of the blue. This key was found in plain view on the floor, right where the slippers had been sitting before being moved during an earlier search.

Further, Kucharski, a deputy in the Calumet County Sheriff's Department, did not even locate the key, as the complaint had alleged. Although he first testified that "we found a key," he quickly admitted that the key was discovered by agents of the Manitowoc Sheriff's Department[12]—the law enforcement agency that was a defendant in Avery's civil suit and, therefore, was not even supposed to be involved in the Halbach investigation.

So, given this, shouldn't the preliminary hearing have identified and prevented a "hasty, malicious, improvident and oppressive prosecution" by the state? And shouldn't the judge have dismissed the case? Not by a long shot. The first problem is that, even if the state were to somehow lose the preliminary hearing, it could simply refile the case and get a fresh kick at the cat—typically, as many kicks as it wants.[13] In this regard, then, the preliminary hearing does little to advance the grandiose vision expressed in Wisconsin court decisions.

But second, it turns out that the state rarely needs that second (or third or fourth) kick at the cat. The reason is the preliminary hearing's burden of proof. What, exactly, is the burden of proof? Is it proof beyond a reasonable doubt, as it is supposed to be at the criminal trial? Is it proof by clear and convincing evidence? How about proof by the preponderance of the evidence, like in a civil case? The answer is none of the above.

Instead, the proof required for the state to win a preliminary hearing and get bindover—that is, to keep the case moving along—is the same as it is for the criminal complaint: probable cause.[14] And just as the state does not have to set forth all of the facts in the complaint, neither does it have to present all of the evidence at the preliminary hearing.[15] Similarly, the facts the state chooses to introduce at the hearing do not have to establish probable cause; once again, the judge will be allowed to draw inferences from those facts.[16] Worse yet, evidence that benefits the defendant must be ignored; the judge must find probable cause, and the "defendant must be bound over for trial even if an equally-believable account points to the defendant's innocence."[17]

If that's the law, then what good is the preliminary hearing at weeding out bogus cases "to save the defendant from the humiliation and anxiety involved in public prosecution"? And if there is

an "equally-believable account that points to the defendant's innocence," then isn't that the exact definition of a "hasty, malicious,
improvident [or] oppressive prosecution"? Isn't that yet another
thing the preliminary hearing is supposed to prevent?

And wasn't Avery's case even stronger than that? After all, the testifying deputy said that Avery's slippers were moved and the key was
not there. Then, the Manitowoc Sheriff's Department claims to have
discovered the key, in that exact location, but only after multiple,
additional entries into Avery's room—a highly unlikely story, to put
it kindly, which is explored in detail in chapter 3.

In other words, had the key really been there, law enforcement
would have seen it the first time they moved the slippers. And even in
the near-impossible scenario that they all went temporarily blind to
the key's presence, it was an agent of the Manitowoc Sheriff's Department who found the key. This agency, recall, had a conflict of interest
as it was a defendant in Avery's multimillion-dollar civil suit and had
a motive to see him convicted. In light of all of this, shouldn't the
judge have dismissed Avery's case after the preliminary hearing?

PLAUSIBILITY VERSUS CREDIBILITY

Even when the state's evidence was collected by biased witnesses—or,
in Avery's case, by an agency with an obvious conflict of interest and
a financial incentive to see him convicted—the law has developed a
hyper-technical distinction between credibility and plausibility that
allows the state's case to live on and move forward.

More specifically, the purpose of the preliminary hearing is to
test the "plausibility" of the state's case, not the "credibility" of its
witnesses.[18] This plausibility-credibility distinction is really just a legal
fiction. "Not surprisingly," then, "Wisconsin courts have struggled
with this distinction, which has bedeviled Anglo-American criminal
procedure for over two hundred years."[19]

If judges haven't been able to figure out the plausibility-credibility
distinction in two hundred years' time, Avery's Wisconsin judge wasn't
likely to do so by the end of his preliminary hearing. But, to succinctly
sum up the plausibility-credibility distinction in plain language, a

witness's truthfulness (credibility) is not an issue at the preliminary hearing; rather, his truthfulness will be assumed. Then, the only question is whether the state's theory of the case is a plausible one.

In Avery's case, consider how a hypothetical, fair-minded, and conscientious judge would analyze the Halbach car key evidence presented at the preliminary hearing. Would he bind the case over for further proceedings or dismiss it? The well-intentioned, hypothetical judge's legal analysis might have gone something like this:

> Had the key been where the Manitowoc Sheriff's Department said it was—in plain view on the floor of Avery's bedroom—they would have found it when they moved his slippers during their previous searches. So they are probably lying about this. But the law does not let me consider the witness's *credibility*; rather, I must assume they are telling the truth.
>
> But the Manitowoc Sheriff's Department was, at the time of their search, a defendant in Avery's civil lawsuit. They had a conflict of interest, were not even supposed to be searching his home, and had a financial motive to see Avery convicted. And I *am* allowed to consider a witness's *motive* at a preliminary hearing.[20]
>
> However, I can't figure out the difference between motive and credibility! And if I consider their motive, it would only be for the purposes of deciding their credibility—which the law clearly says I can't do! To hell with it: I find that it is plausible that agents of the Manitowoc Sheriff's Department were searching Avery's bedroom, found a key on the floor, and that key belonged to Halbach's car. I therefore bind this case over for further proceedings.

But most judges have never pondered the plausibility-credibility distinction, or the difference between credibility and motive. And most judges don't engage in an inner struggle when making their decisions. Rather, even fair-minded judges will simply find probable cause after nearly every preliminary hearing, and will routinely bind defendants over for further proceedings.

The preliminary hearing failed to protect Steven Avery from the "expense," "humiliation," and "anxiety" of a "hasty" and "improvident" prosecution. And the hearing is equally useless to nearly every criminal defendant. In fact, the hearing is so close to meaningless that there was recently a strong push to abolish it altogether. Although this movement failed, the Wisconsin legislature, in 2011, changed the law to water down the preliminary hearing even further by permitting the state to use hearsay to obtain bindover.[21] Now, the preliminary hearing is virtually indistinguishable from the criminal complaint: both are governed by the probable cause standard, and, even at the preliminary hearing, that probable cause determination can be based on hearsay—including multiple levels of hearsay.[22]

In essence, while preliminary hearings still involve a live witness, that witness typically knows very little about the case beyond having read the complaint. Prosecutors will rarely, if ever, call witnesses who actually know something about the alleged crime; rather, their witness will merely repeat what someone else told her—or, more commonly, what someone else *told someone else* who told her.

But can't the defendant simply call those witnesses himself? Even though Wisconsin statutory law specifically grants defendants the right to call their own witnesses at the preliminary hearing,[23] courts rarely, if ever, allow them to do so.[24] The courts' reasoning often goes as follows. Once the state finishes with its evidence, probable cause has already been established. Therefore, even if the defense witness were to make a highly credible case for innocence, the test is one of plausibility, not credibility, and all inferences must go to the state. Therefore, the court would have to bind the case over anyway. This renders the defense witnesses meaningless, so there is no point in allowing defendants to exercise their statutory right to call witnesses in the first place.

This creates a bizarre, illogical conundrum that is quite fitting for the irrational body of law governing preliminary hearings: the defendant has the statutory right to call witnesses at the preliminary hearing, but only in cases where the state's witnesses cannot establish probable cause. Of course, in that situation, the defendant would never get the opportunity to call his witnesses. Why not? Because if the state wasn't able to establish probable cause, the judge would have to dismiss the case. The courts have, essentially, erased the defendant's statutory right to call witnesses from Wisconsin's statute book. (This is judicial activism in its purest form, yet it will never earn the attention of the national, or even local, media outlets.)

But worse than being nearly meaningless, the preliminary hearing, as Avery learned, can actually cause defendants substantial harm.

STACKING THE CHARGES

When the state of Wisconsin charges a defendant with a misdemeanor crime, the defendant is not entitled to a preliminary hearing. Rather, if the complaint sets forth probable cause for the misdemeanor, that is sufficient, and the defendant must stand trial (or strike a plea bargain, or somehow win a dismissal on other grounds).

In a felony case, however, we saw that not only must there be probable cause in the complaint, but the defendant is also entitled to a preliminary hearing that, in theory, promises additional protection for felony defendants. We also saw that, in practice, this promise is an empty one. But worse yet, and quite paradoxically, the preliminary hearing actually results in the felony defendant enjoying fewer safeguards than the defendant charged with a mere misdemeanor crime.

Here's how it works. Assume that a defendant is charged with misdemeanor disorderly conduct for swearing at a family member during an argument—a very common criminal charge in Wisconsin. Further assume that, a few weeks into the case, the state decides to add a charge of misdemeanor battery, even though the probable cause section of the complaint only alleges that the defendant swore. In this case, the defendant could move to dismiss the battery charge because probable cause was not established in the complaint. That is, the complaint does not allege that the defendant touched, let alone caused physical pain or injury to, his family member.

That is essentially what happened to Avery in the Halbach case, only with more serious charges. The state first charged him with murder and mutilating a corpse. A preliminary hearing was held, and Avery was bound over for trial. Then, the state decided to stack on additional charges, adding sexual assault, kidnapping, and false imprisonment. Avery's defense team argued that "[n]o reliable information supports any of the three new charges; they accordingly fail to establish *probable cause*, and should be dismissed."[25]

The state opposed this motion, and the court decided in the state's favor and permitted it to add the new charges.[26] Why? Because in Wisconsin, even though the probable cause standard governs the criminal complaint and the preliminary hearing in a felony case, once a preliminary hearing has been conducted, the probable cause standard falls away and is replaced with an even lower standard known as the transactional-relation test.

First, and rather bizarrely, the judge can bind the defendant over after a preliminary hearing if he believes there is probable cause that "a felony" was committed, even if the state never charged the particular felony the judge has in mind.[27] But second, once a defendant is bound over on "a felony," the state is free to add as many additional charges as it wishes, even without any probable cause in the complaint, and even without any probable cause having been adduced at the preliminary hearing. Instead, the only requirement is that the new charges are "transactionally related" to the original charges; that is, they must not be "wholly unrelated to the evidence which was already presented at the preliminary hearing."[28]

This new, easier transactional-relation test hinges on whether the new charges are "related in terms of parties involved, geographical proximity, time, physical evidence, motive and intent."[29] In Avery's Halbach case, adding on the new counts, including sexual assault, kidnapping, and false imprisonment, were slam dunks under this test. Because the new charges related to the Halbach murder, and allegedly occurred on Avery's property within hours of the murder, they easily satisfied the transactional-relation test. Therefore, Avery's defense team's argument that there was no probable cause to support the new charges, while true, did not persuade the court.

Such charge-stacking would never have been allowed had Avery been charged in a misdemeanor case, where the probable cause standard does *not* get replaced with the transactional-relation test. Rather, with a misdemeanor, the probable cause standard remains intact until the higher burden of proof takes effect at the jury trial.[30]

Ultimately, in Avery's case, the add-on charges were dismissed much later in the proceedings—but only after the defense spent a tremendous amount of time, financial resources, and energy fighting them,[31] and after the prosecutor publicized the charges to the media and represented them as the gospel truth.[32] In short, the damage was done, even though the state's unfounded criminal charges never formally made it to the jury.

The state's real goal in stacking up charges without probable cause—a task made easy by the preliminary hearing and the transactional-relation test—was to give the jury multiple counts from which to choose. Because felonies carry such staggeringly high penalties, the state is a big winner if it can get the jury to split the verdict and convict the defendant of just one or two of the counts.

The state did achieve this goal: it won a split verdict against Avery. And it accomplished this even after its stacked-on charges—sexual assault, kidnapping, and false imprisonment—were eventually dismissed. That is, the state won its split verdict because of its earlier, more modest charge-stacking in the original complaint where it charged not only murder, but also mutilating a corpse. This second count turned out to be incredibly important. Why? Because the prosecutor never actually persuaded the jury of Avery's guilt. Rather, the prosecutor merely obtained a nonsensical compromise verdict, but the compromise served the state's purpose just the same. As the defense argued in its post-conviction motion for a new trial,

> The jury convicted Avery on . . . first degree intentional homicide, but acquitted him on . . . mutilation of a corpse. Those verdicts are *inconsistent and irreconcilable.* The State abandoned its party to a crime theory during trial, and presented no evidence of the involvement of any other actor in either crime. Then, in closing argument, the State argued that all the evidence showed that *one man and one man only* was responsible for the two crimes. There was no rational basis on which to find that Avery killed Teresa Halbach, but did not also mutilate her body by gunshot wounds to the head or by burning it.[33]

The defense was forced to concede, however, that Wisconsin courts tolerate such irrational, split verdicts—at least in criminal cases. In civil cases, where there is often corporate money at stake, the corporate defendant who is victimized by a compromise verdict *may* be entitled to a new trial.[34] But a criminal defendant like Avery does not have such protection under the law. The state's two-count charge-stacking in the original complaint served its purpose. It led to a nonsensical, mixed jury verdict that the court upheld. This, of course, only proves the wisdom of the prosecutor's charging strategy: more counts are better, and sometimes even two counts will do the trick.

WAIVING THE PRELIMINARY HEARING

Could Avery have avoided these problems by waiving, instead of having, his preliminary hearing in the Halbach murder case?[35] Wouldn't waiving the hearing have prevented the state from stacking on additional charges under the transactional-relation test?[36] In theory, yes, trouble could have been averted by strategically waiving the preliminary hearing.[37] But once again, theory and practice do not always align in criminal courts.

It is true that, under Wisconsin's bizarre law, "once the defendant has been bound over for trial on at least one count relating to the transaction, the prosecutor may . . . charge additional counts not wholly unrelated."[38] However, the court went on to say, "We construe the . . . phrase 'once the defendant has been bound over for trial' to assume a bindover that is supported by the *evidence adduced at the preliminary hearing.*"[39]

This, of course, is logical. If Avery had waived his preliminary hearing, how could the new, add-on charges of sexual assault, kidnapping, and false imprisonment be transactionally related (or "not wholly unrelated") to evidence that was *never presented* because no hearing was held? The answer to this question is obvious: they cannot be. Therefore, had Avery waived his preliminary hearing, the probable cause standard never would have fallen away, and never would have been replaced by the much easier transactional-relation test. And because the new, add-on charges were not supported by probable cause, they would have to be dismissed.

Unfortunately, however, given the irrationality of the body of law governing preliminary hearings, few trial judges understand this distinction. Most will metaphorically throw up their arms and assume the state is legally permitted to file whatever charges it wishes, even when the preliminary hearing has been waived.[40] Even more unfortunate, it is an uphill battle to educate trial judges on the nuances of probable cause and transactional relation. And the full cost of this judicial education would fall solely on the defense. In the real world, this cost is simply more than most defendants can afford to spend in lawyers' fees, and more than busy lawyers like Buting and Strang can afford in terms of time and energy—particularly in light of the larger issues they faced on a daily basis when defending Steven Avery.

Chapter 10

BAIL OR JAIL?

"They just don't want me out."

—Steven Avery

In the Penny Beerntsen case, Steven Avery was denied bail. In the Teresa Halbach case, Avery's bail was as high as $750,000 cash after Dassey's alleged confession implicated him in the murder. In Wisconsin, unlike other states, the defendant or his family must post the entire bail amount set by the court.[1] And although it is legally possible to post real estate instead of cash,[2] the judge denied the Avery family's request for a property bond. As a result, Avery sat in jail for more than one year before the Halbach trial started—and he has been in custody ever since.

But what is the purpose of bail? Why was Avery's bail so high? And, more important, did keeping Avery in custody during the course of the case help the state win the jury trial?

ASSURING THE DEFENDANT'S APPEARANCE

The purpose of bail is to make sure the defendant shows up for court. And because the defendant is presumed innocent of the allegations, bail may not be used to "protect the public." Rather, to protect the public and even specific individuals from possible harm, the court may impose non-monetary conditions of release. For example, a court may order that the defendant not possess a firearm or other weapons, may not drink alcohol, or may not have any contact with certain places, individuals, or even classes of individuals such as children. These and similar non-monetary conditions "may be imposed for the purpose of protecting members of the community from serious bodily harm or preventing the intimidation of witnesses."[3]

Cash bail, on the other hand, "may be imposed . . . only upon a finding by the court that there is a reasonable basis to believe that bail is necessary *to assure appearance in court*."[4] With regard to the amount, "[i]f bail is imposed, it shall be *only in the amount found necessary* to assure the appearance of the defendant."[5] And when deciding what is necessary, the factors that a judge may consider include the defendant's financial resources and his place of residence.[6] For example, if the defendant happens to be a rich, jet-setting New Yorker who was only visiting Wisconsin when he allegedly committed the crime, he would have little incentive to return to America's dairy land for court. Therefore, his bail should be higher than that of a poor, working-class, lifelong Wisconsin resident who is charged with the same crime.

So why was Steven Avery's bail set as high as $750,000 in the Halbach case? Was he somehow considered a flight risk? In a motion asking the court to lower the amount of bail, Dean Strang argued,

> Mr. Avery was born in Manitowoc County. His parents were born in Manitowoc County. Almost all of his nieces, nephews, brothers, sisters, children, and parents live in Manitowoc County. He has lived in Manitowoc County his entire life, save the 18 years that the State of Wisconsin wrongfully required him to live in prisons located far from his home. *There is no reason to think that he will flee Manitowoc County if conditionally released on bond*, particularly given the financial loss that would befall his family if he failed to comply with conditions of bond.[7]

In addition to Avery's lifelong residence and family ties, there was even stronger evidence that he was not a flight risk: his actual behavior before his arrest. More specifically, when Halbach was declared missing, Avery talked to the sheriffs and even let them onto his property to look for her—*twice*. Then, when the sheriffs got a warrant, searched Avery's property for an eight-day stretch, and prevented him from returning to his home, he still did not flee. Instead, he stayed at his family's nearby Wisconsin property, even though he feared that he would soon be wrongfully arrested and prosecuted—*again*. And all of these facts were undisputed. In an early news conference in *Making a Murderer*, government officials even admitted that Avery was in the immediate area and was fully cooperating with their investigation.

So given that Avery was not a flight risk—something he proved beyond any doubt by staying put even after the cops placed him in their crosshairs—why did the judge impose such a high cash bail? The reason is that, despite a bail's stated, legal purpose of ensuring that the defendant shows up for court, the government reaps tremendous benefits by keeping a defendant locked up before trial.

LET'S MAKE A DEAL

Most criminal cases aren't nearly as serious as Steven Avery's. In fact, due to ever-expanding criminal codes, the majority of criminal cases consist of charges like disorderly conduct, simple marijuana possession, criminal battery that caused pain (but no visible injury), child abuse for spanking, retail theft, carrying a concealed weapon (even when no one was attacked or threatened), driving with a suspended license, issuing bad checks, or any one of the dozens of other crimes that don't involve an actual injury or substantial harm of any kind.

Yet despite the relatively minor nature of most criminal cases, judges often impose cash bail on defendants, thereby forcing them to sit in jail while their cases are pending.[8] This, in turn, gives the state a tremendous amount of leverage: the prosecutor can make a plea offer to resolve the case for probation, which would let the defendant out of jail in the short term while keeping him in "the system" for years to come. This promise of immediate release from custody is often too much to resist; therefore, most defendants choose this option rather than sitting in jail for months, or even years, awaiting their trial date.[9] And even if the defendant is strong enough to resist the lure of immediate freedom, and instead goes to trial and is acquitted, the state still comes out a winner because it will have incarcerated the defendant for months or years before setting him free, thus obtaining the functional equivalent of a jail sentence (but without a conviction).

In serious cases like Avery's, of course, probation is not a realistic possibility. However, in such cases, locking the defendant up before trial provides even greater advantages for the state.

HAMPERING THE DEFENSE

In Avery's case, being incarcerated before trial made it incredibly difficult for him to assist his lawyers in building a defense. As Dean Strang wrote in Avery's bond motion, with Avery locked up "he cannot review police reports in privacy," or "assist counsel by showing counsel . . . relevant places and things on the Avery Salvage property. . . ."[10]

Further, even when Strang and Buting were working on the case in their offices, they would have strongly preferred Avery to be out of custody. That way, they could have simply called him on the phone or summoned him to their offices when they had questions. But with Avery incarcerated, phone calls may be recorded—more on that later—or, at a minimum, must be scheduled ahead of time. And when they wanted to meet with Avery in person, they had to drive long distances to the jail and were allowed to see him only for limited periods during specified hours.

In a complex, fact-intensive case like Avery's, having a client locked up before trial is a tremendous disadvantage—a disadvantage that any prosecutor would be eager to impose on the defendant's counsel. But this government perk of pretrial incarceration pales by comparison to the other benefits reaped by the state.

INTIMIDATION OF WITNESSES

With Avery locked up before trial, government investigators had a much easier time isolating and intimidating his potential defense witnesses. For example, before trial the cops targeted Avery's fiancée possibly to destroy Avery's relationship with her and turn her against him. Why? Because shortly after Halbach was killed, Avery was on the phone with his fiancée who was in jail for her drunk driving case. Their discussion could have been relevant evidence, as she could have testified that Avery was *not* breathless, hurried, excited, or upset when he called her. Such a calm demeanor, of course, would *not* be consistent with a person who had just committed a violent murder and was frantically trying to hide the evidence and burn the corpse.

Even though Avery's phone call with his fiancée was not overwhelming evidence of innocence—it would have been, at best, a small part of the defense—the cops still targeted the fiancée to pressure her to turn on Avery. *Making a Murderer* showed one video-recorded meeting where the investigator tried to convince her, much like a prosecutor would try to convince a jury, of Avery's guilt:

> Think what he did to that girl. Sit and think about that for a minute. Think about her family. . . . *By sticking up for him, what does that make you look like?* He killed her. He killed her. . . . Think about that. . . . That's the kind of person you want to spend the rest of your life with?[11]

Destroying Avery's relationships and turning people against him can more easily be accomplished, of course, when he is locked up, cut off from the outside world, and unable to regularly communicate with his friends, family, and witnesses. And turnabout is *not* fair play: while the cops are permitted to strong-arm the defendant's witnesses—the cop in *Making a Murderer* had no qualms about video recording himself when bullying Avery's fiancée—a defendant who is wealthy enough to post bail will be ordered, as a condition of his bond, not to harass or intimidate witnesses.[12] Often, the defendant will be prohibited from having any contact whatsoever with codefendants and potential witnesses—assuming the prosecutor knows the witnesses' names at the time of the bond hearing and is alert enough to request the no-contact order from the court. And if the defendant violates any of his bond conditions, including any no-contact orders, he can be charged criminally—even when his conduct, by itself, would not otherwise be a crime.[13]

As *Making a Murderer* demonstrated, the cops' intimidation tactics paid off in a big way. Although their attempts to bully Avery's fiancée did not bear much fruit, they next turned their attention to Brendan Dassey, a much easier target. And while their initial goal was merely to get Dassey to change his story and incriminate Avery, they soon realized they had struck gold: they easily convinced Dassey to incriminate himself in the Halbach murder.

PHONE CALLS

Avery's pretrial incarceration also provided the state with access to his telephone calls—a huge advantage the state would not have enjoyed had Avery been able to post bail. And while it was theoretically possible for Avery to avoid using the phone while in custody, this simply was not realistic. To understand this, we need to understand the psychological effects of isolation—a common tactic used in numerous contexts by those in power: "Police investigators typically isolate suspects from family and friends before an interrogation begins. Military interrogators isolate suspected terrorists, [and] religious cults often isolate their members. . . . Social isolation within unfamiliar surroundings leads to anxiety and a desire to remove one's self from an uncomfortable situation."[14]

Removing someone from his home, and then locking him in a cage, most certainly "leads to anxiety." But unless the defendant is wealthy enough to post bail, he will not be able "to remove [him]self" from the horrors of confinement. Instead, to cope with this highly "uncomfortable situation," defendants typically seek as much contact as possible with friends and family through jail visits and phone calls. The problem, however, is that Big Brother is watching, listening, and recording. "The Calumet County Jail tape records every telephone call that Steven Avery or any other inmate makes. It also records every visit with an inmate, other than lawyer-client contact visits. In Avery's case, the state even tapes at least some meetings with his pastor."[15]

Of course, after the government recorded Avery's phone calls, the prosecutor wanted to use them at trial. Why? Because as we saw in the Penny Beerntsen case twenty years earlier, even innocent statements can be creatively interpreted as evidence of guilt. And sometimes, such creative interpretation is not even necessary. For example, in Dassey's case, the interrogators instructed him to call his mother on the phone, from the jail, to discuss his case. As Lawrence White explained in an earlier part of *Making a Murderer*, Dassey "didn't really understand the precariousness of his own position."[16] Because of this, he quickly took the interrogators' bait and called her. And those recorded jail phone calls were probably the most convincing evidence the state produced at Dassey's trial. The phone calls, of course, never would have been made, let alone recorded, had Dassey's family been able to post his bail.

JAILHOUSE SNITCHES

The benefits of pretrial incarceration continued to roll in for the state. In addition to hampering the defense lawyers' trial preparation, intimidating Avery's witnesses, and recording Dassey's phone call confessions to his mother, the state was also able to tap one of its most valuable resources: other inmates.

But what if the high-profile defendant like Avery is in custody, every inmate in the cellblock wants to be his best friend. Why? Because those inmates are facing charges of their own. And if an inmate can somehow help the state convict a white whale like Avery, then that inmate can win tremendous concessions in return—including the dismissal of some or all of his own charges. How does an inmate accomplish this? By turning into a jailhouse snitch. The inmate will cozy up to the high-profile defendant, get him talking, and then call the prosecutor's office to repeat everything he said.

But what if the high-profile defendant doesn't say anything? Or what if he simply tells the snitch that he is innocent? It doesn't really matter. The snitch can simply twist the defendant's words, take his words out of context, or even misquote him. We saw this phenomenon in the Penny Beerntsen case, but in a different context. In the Beerntsen case, the sheriffs testified at trial that, when arresting Avery, they only told him he was being arrested for "attempted murder"; however, Avery allegedly responded to this news by asking "where the lady lived."[17] This statement was used as evidence of Avery's guilt at trial and throughout the appeals process—after all, how could Avery have known the victim was a "lady" unless he was the real perpetrator?

This example demonstrates how evidence of guilt can be conjured up from absolutely nothing. That is, we now know for sure that Avery was innocent, so his words were either twisted—for example, maybe he really asked where the *victim* lived—or they were taken out of context— for example, maybe the sheriffs actually told him he was being arrested for the attempted murder *of Penny Beerntsen.* Or maybe the entire thing was fabricated; perhaps Avery never said anything at all.

If the sheriffs were willing to twist Avery's words, take them out of context, or even create them out of whole cloth, what do you think jailhouse snitches would be willing to do if it meant getting their own charges dismissed or reduced? Dean Strang, no doubt, had this in mind when he drafted Avery's bond motion. In the motion, Strang argued that, as long as Avery remains in custody, he "cannot review police reports in privacy."[18]

More specifically, this is Strang's concern: if he and Buting were to give Avery a copy of the police reports, jailhouse snitches would get their hands on them, read them, and then call the prosecutor to report that Avery confessed to things contained in the reports. For example, if one of Avery's police reports stated that Halbach had been shot "in the head," then the snitch would tell the prosecutor that Avery confessed to him that he shot Halbach "in the head." Then, at trial, the prosecutor will argue, "How else could Mr. Jailhouse Snitch have known this if Avery did not confess it to him?" To complete the argument, the jailhouse snitch will testify that he never saw Avery's police reports, that he knows this information only because Avery confessed it to him, and that getting his own charges dismissed has in no way influenced his testimony. Rather, he came forward simply because it was the right thing to do.

This line of evidence then leads to a trial within the trial. If the defendant is lucky, the judge will understand the law and will let the defense lawyer cross-examine the snitch on why the snitch was in custody, how many charges he was facing, and what he expected to get in exchange for his testimony. In this best-case scenario, the defense will spend a tremendous amount of time and effort simply to dig out of this hole and get back to ground level.

On the other hand, if the defendant is not lucky, the judge won't understand the law or the importance of such cross-examination, and won't let the defense lawyer challenge the snitch's credibility. In this worst-case scenario, the snitch's testimony will bolster the state's case, and could severely damage the defendant's chances of an acquittal.

But did snitches really play a role in Avery's case? Absolutely, and here's how. Brendan Dassey first made a statement to the cops, and then Ken Kratz repeated it to the media in lurid detail, thus making it widely and publicly known. In this statement, Dassey allegedly claimed that Avery stabbed and slashed Halbach in the trailer before dragging her outside. However, the state had a problem: there was not a single drop of her blood anywhere to be found on Avery's property. Fortunately, a jailhouse snitch was ready, willing, and able to help the state explain away this inconvenient fact. After an investigator visited with the snitch, also known as the "informant," the investigator wrote,

INFORMANT stated to us over the last few weeks, he had been talking with STEVEN AVERY who is in the same cellblock as INFORMANT. According to INFORMANT, they were talking about a bonfire and STEVEN had told INFORMANT that his nieces and nephews were supposed to come to his house on the weekend for the fire. STEVEN also mentioned to INFORMANT about burning four tires and INFORMANT stated to me he thought that was weird to burn that amount of tires if you were going to have kids around the fire. STEVEN also told INFORMANT that BRENDAN was the only one at the fire with him.[19]

That's very nice of this jailhouse snitch to be concerned about the children who might be placed in harm's way from Avery burning too many tires at one time. But what else did the snitch have to say? Did he know anything about Halbach's murder, perhaps? Maybe something to corroborate Dassey's now public statement about cutting and slashing Halbach into a bloody mess in Avery's bedroom?

INFORMANT went on to say that when they talked again, STEVEN told him that STEVEN's girlfriend had told STEVEN that the police had found blood on the headboard that was located in his bedroom. STEVEN also told INFORMANT the police would not find anything on the mattress. INFORMANT stated to STEVEN at that time the only way there would not be any blood there was if you had cleaned it with bleach or if you had plastic over the mattress. INFORMANT stated after he had said this to STEVEN, STEVEN stopped talking to him.[20]

Excellent! Just what the state needed: Avery's quasi-confession, made through his silence in the face of the snitch's statement that he must have used a plastic mattress cover or bleach. Surely, an innocent person would have vehemently denied using, or even owning, a plastic mattress cover or a bottle of bleach. Avery's failure to do so is therefore evidence of his guilt.

But why was this snitch trying to curry the state's favor? What kind of charges was he facing? How was he hoping to help himself? That was the strange part because the defense could find no reason for him to even be in custody in the first place. This prompted the defense team to write,

Steven Avery requests an inquiry on the record into the reasons for the presence of INFORMANT in the Calumet County Jail with Mr. Avery. He also gives notice that he will consider any further state inquiry of INFORMANT about statements allegedly made by Mr. Avery about the pending charges to be deliberate elicitation of information [by the state] from Mr. Avery, contrary to his federal and state constitutional rights to counsel.[21]

The real lesson is that, if you are incarcerated before trial, anything you say—whether to another inmate, through a jail phone call, or during a jail visit from someone—can be twisted or taken out of context. And even if you don't say anything, someone might make something up. And even if that someone admits that you were silent and "stopped talking to him," this, too, could be evidence of guilt. You're damned if you do . . .

JAIL, NOT BAIL

At the initial appearance in Avery's case for the Halbach murder, the judge could have—and some would argue should have—said something like this:

> All right, Mr. Avery, you were accused once before, and the sheriffs, the prosecutor, the judge, the jury, the victim, and the public were all convinced of your guilt. It turns out we got that one wrong, and it cost you eighteen years of your life. (Sorry about that, by the way.) And now you're accused again, but these are all the same government agencies in this case as in the last case. So I am going to presume your innocence in this case. On top of all of that, you have proven that you are not a flight risk, as you stayed in the immediate area while law enforcement searched your home for an eight-day span. You had plenty of opportunity to flee, but you didn't. So I'm going to set your bail at only $100,000 cash. In the alternative, I'll allow your parents to post all of their real estate instead of the $100,000 cash. If you skip town and don't appear for trial, they'll lose their property and will have nothing. Do you understand that?

Of course, the judge didn't say that. But how could the judge have justified the $750,000 cash bail? Ironically, the single most important factor in determining the bail amount is actually within the prosecutor's control, "the nature, number and gravity of the offenses and the potential penalty the defendant faces. . . ."[22] So the more serious the accusation that the prosecutor can muster, and the greater number of charges he can stack on top of each other, the more likely the bail will be high and the defendant will remain incarcerated pending trial.

And another big factor in setting bail, ironically, is "whether the defendant has been bound over for trial after a preliminary examination. . . ."[23] We learned in chapter 9 that bindover is incredibly easy for the state to obtain. With the low burden of proof and all inferences going to the state, it would be a real feat not to win bindover. Further, once the state obtains bindover, the transactional-relation test allows it to file additional felonies without any probable cause in the complaint.

In sum, there is a massive snowball effect at work when determining a defendant's bail. Even one felony charge is serious and will justify a high cash bail. The felony charge also requires a preliminary hearing, after which bindover of the defendant is all but guaranteed. This bindover is, in itself, another factor contributing to a high cash bail. And once bindover is achieved, more felony charges can be added, even without probable cause in the complaint. These additional charges, of course, are factors that justify setting the cash bail even higher.

So what started atop the metaphoric hill as a presumption of innocence rolled downhill, built up steam, and snowballed into a $750,000 cash bail by the time it reached the bottom. This high cash bail meant that Avery was forced to remain in custody while awaiting trial. And, as this chapter has demonstrated, his pretrial incarceration provided many advantages to the state and played (at least) a small part in turning the Wisconsin state prison system into Avery's permanent home.

Chapter 11

INTRODUCTION TO LEGAL ETHICS

"Ethics, schmethics. "[1]

C hapters 12 and 13 deal, broadly speaking, with some of the lawyer ethics issues in *Making a Murderer*. Chapter 12 discusses some of the ethics rules that apply to the criminal defense lawyer. Chapter 13 discusses the prosecutor's dual role as an advocate for the state and a so-called "minister of justice." Both sets of rules, it turns out, played a fairly large role in the government's wins against Avery and Dassey. But to fully appreciate the next two chapters, a very brief, general discussion of legal ethics will be helpful.

THE BODY OF LAW

Lawyer ethics in Wisconsin, and in all other states, consist of a disorganized and convoluted collection of (1) general ethical principles; (2) highly specific ethics rules; (3) numerous delineated exceptions to the rules; (4) commentary to the rules; and (5) countless ethics opinions and court cases. The ethics opinions and court cases attempt—usually without success—to apply or reconcile the often incomprehensible and sometimes conflicting principles, rules, exceptions, and comments. In short, the body of law on legal ethics is an indecipherable and unmitigated disaster. And it is long. Wisconsin's unwieldy law spans two parts and *168 pages*—and that does not include a single interpretive ethics opinion or court case.[2]

In addition to being incomprehensible, this body of law is simultaneously too suffocating and too lax. For an example of an ethics rule being too suffocating, consider rule 1.9. According to Wisconsin's Office of Lawyer Regulation (OLR) and the Wisconsin State Bar, this rule prohibits an attorney from discussing *any* information relating to a former client's case—even when that information is widely and publicly available, and even when the attorney wants to discuss the information in a pro-client manner.[3]

For example, suppose I represented a client at criminal trial and the client was convicted. The client then hired an appellate lawyer to appeal the conviction. A couple of years later, the appellate court publishes its decision: the jury's verdict and the conviction are reversed. This appellate court decision is, of course, public information. In fact, Wisconsin appellate and supreme court decisions even use a public domain citation system. And unlike decades past where an interested person had to drive to the courthouse to view or copy public information, this appellate court decision is easily and freely available, to anyone in the world, via multiple websites.

Despite this, rule 1.9—or, more accurately, the OLR's and Wisconsin State Bar's irrational interpretation of the horrifically worded rule 1.9—says that I may not discuss the appellate court decision because, even though it is public information and even though I was not the lawyer handling the appeal, it is still "information relating to the representation" of my former client.[4] Therefore, according to the OLR and Wisconsin State Bar, I cannot tell others about the decision, discuss the decision at a legal education seminar, or even speak about the decision in a pro-client manner. In fact, both Wisconsin bureaucracies contend that my discussion of this published case would somehow be disloyal to my former client. (Their mistake, of course, is confusing loyalty with silence.)

This particular ethics rule is incredibly draconian. If the OLR and Wisconsin State Bar were correct, it perpetually bans my speech for all purposes and with regard to all information, including widely and publicly available information, simply because I once represented the defendant. Meanwhile, every other person in the world has the right to talk freely about this public information.

I have written extensively about the absurdity of this ethics rule,[5] and have also petitioned the Supreme Court of Wisconsin to clarify the rule in order to protect Wisconsin lawyers from our own bar association and the OLR.[6] But my purpose in using this example here is not to demonstrate the uselessness (or even the harmfulness) of the OLR and Wisconsin State Bar, or the absurdity of ethics rule 1.9. Rather, my purpose is to demonstrate that lawyer ethics rules can be incredibly harsh, uncompromising, and unforgiving—even with regard to constitutionally protected attorney speech about public information that in no imaginable way harms the client, the public, or the legal profession.

Given this hard-line approach to legal ethics, one would expect that the ethics rules are equally draconian when it comes to important things, such as a defense attorney's and prosecutor's conduct in high-profile homicide cases. Unfortunately, as the next two chapters demonstrate, that is not the case. While the ethics system can be incredibly suffocating when it comes to things that do not matter—thus allowing the OLR and the Wisconsin State Bar to maintain the illusion of protecting clients from their attorneys—the ethics system is toothless and ineffective when it comes to what really matters: ensuring fair trials for clients accused of crimes.

DON'T HATE THE PLAYER

Before we dive into defense lawyer and prosecutor ethics in the next two chapters, it is important to remember that, just as in the other chapters, my goal is to demonstrate how a particular aspect of "the system" contributed to Avery's and Dassey's convictions. And while the next two chapters will certainly discuss many of the statements and actions of defense lawyer Len Kachinsky and prosecutor Ken Kratz, my purpose is *not* to claim that either lawyer behaved unethically. In fact, my conclusion is that, under the rules, both lawyers acted ethically and, in Kachinsky's case, "effectively"—more on that term in the next chapter.

I base my conclusions about Kachinsky and Kratz on two things. First, given the vague language, subtle nuances, countless exceptions, and conflicting interpretations that plague nearly every ethics rule and legal standard governing attorney performance, an attorney's actions that might appear to violate a rule or legal standard could easily turn out *not* to be a violation. Second, and more important, to my knowledge there was never a finding that Kachinsky or Kratz—or any lawyer in the documentary—violated any ethics rule or legal standard governing attorney performance. (Ken Kratz was disciplined for a rule violation—an interesting topic discussed in chapter 13—but that disciplinary action was not related to his prosecution of Avery or Dassey.)

If my position, then, is that Kachinsky and Kratz did not violate any ethics rules or legal standards in the defense or prosecution of either Avery or Dassey, then what is the point of the next two chapters? The point, again, is that the system—in this case, Wisconsin's system of lawyer ethics as it relates to criminal law—failed to protect Avery's and Dassey's right to a fair trial. That is, I believe the problem lies not with any of the individual lawyers or "players," but rather with the rules, standards, and referees that make up the system or "the game."

Chapter 12

THE EFFECTIVE ASSISTANCE OF COUNSEL

"That ain't no lawyer as far as I'm concerned. A lawyer is supposed to work for you."

—Allan Avery, Avery's father,
on Brendan Dassey's lawyer

W isconsin's ethics rules start with the basic principle that an attorney must be loyal to his client: "As advocate, a lawyer zealously asserts the client's position under the rules of the adversary system."[1] In doing so, a lawyer must also be diligent and "act with commitment and dedication to the interests of the client. . . ."[2]

When fulfilling the above obligations, a lawyer must be competent, which requires "the legal knowledge, skill, thoroughness and preparation reasonably necessary for the representation."[3] A lawyer is also required to communicate with his client, including "consult[ing] with the client about the means by which the client's objectives are to be accomplished. . . ."[4]

And the ethics rules get even more specific. For example, an attorney must keep his client's confidences, and must "not reveal information relating to the representation" of the client.[5] At a minimum, this means that a defense attorney may not take information that was provided by the client, and then disclose it to the prosecutor for the state to use against the client.

DEFICIENT PERFORMANCE AND PREJUDICE

When a defendant is convicted at trial and then appeals that conviction, the appellate lawyer typically does not accuse the trial lawyer of violating specific, individual ethics principles or rules. Instead, the appellate lawyer will argue that the trial attorney was "ineffective," which comes down to a two-part test.[6]

First, to prove ineffective assistance of counsel, the appellate lawyer must demonstrate that the trial attorney's performance was *deficient*. Deficient performance can take many forms, including violations of the previously described ethics rules. For example, perhaps the trial lawyer was not loyal to the client due to a conflict of interest. Or, despite his best efforts, perhaps the trial lawyer simply was not competent to handle the client's case and therefore wasn't aware that certain defenses were available to him. Or, even if the trial lawyer was aware of all the possible defenses, perhaps he failed to consult with the client to discuss important issues regarding the use of those defenses.

After arguing that the trial attorney's performance was deficient, the appellate lawyer then argues the second prong of the test, that the defendant was *prejudiced* by the deficiency. Prejudice is roughly defined as whether the trial attorney's deficient performance undermines the court's confidence in the jury's guilty verdict.[7]

To briefly illustrate how this test works, suppose that a defendant is accused of criminal battery for a bar fight. He hires a trial attorney who argues self-defense at trial, but the defendant is convicted. After the conviction, the defendant hires an appellate lawyer to file an appeal. During this process, the appellate lawyer discovers that the trial lawyer never filed a "discovery demand" with the prosecutor; as a result, the prosecutor never turned over an eyewitness's written statement. And without the written statement, the trial lawyer didn't know about the witness and therefore never called that witness at trial. When asked about this at the post-conviction hearing, the trial lawyer admitted that he didn't know he had to file a discovery demand to get this information. Failing to file a discovery demand, therefore, could constitute deficient performance because the attorney was not competent or at least was not diligent.

But the next step is for the court to decide whether the trial lawyer's deficient performance prejudiced the defendant. To decide this, the court has to look at the written statement (that the trial lawyer never obtained at the time of trial) and the trial transcript. If, for example, the witness had stated, "I really didn't see how the fight started," then the defendant probably was not prejudiced by his trial lawyer's failure to file the discovery demand, to obtain the written statement, and to call the witness at trial. Why not? Because the witness's testimony would not have supported the defendant's claim of self-defense.

Similarly, even if the witness's statement indicated that the defendant was attacked first and then reacted in self-defense, this might still fail the prejudice prong if, at trial, the trial lawyer had called several other witnesses who testified to that very same thing. If that were the case, the missing witness's testimony may simply have been cumulative to the testimony of other witnesses. Just because the jury chose not to believe those witnesses, and instead convicted the defendant, doesn't mean things would have turned out differently had one more witness testified and said the same thing.

It should be obvious from this example that, when left in judicial hands, this two-prong ineffective assistance of counsel test is highly subjective. And, as we know from chapter 2, judges don't like to give convicted defendants a new trial. So keeping in mind the subjectivity of the two-prong test, coupled with the judicial proclivity to affirm convictions at all costs, let's take a close look at Brendan Dassey's appeal where he challenged the performance of Len Kachinsky.

LEN KACHINSKY, ATTORNEY AT LAW

Dassey's appellate lawyers argued that one of Dassey's pretrial attorneys, Len Kachinsky, "breached the fundamental duty of loyalty"; the appellate court analyzed this claim as a form of "ineffective assistance of counsel."[8] Therefore, the court had to decide whether Kachinsky performed deficiently by acting "to the detriment of the client's interests."[9] And, if he did, the court would then have to decide whether his deficient performance resulted in prejudice, or "demonstrable detriment," to Dassey.[10]

Readers will likely remember the affable, easygoing, youthful-in-appearance, media-friendly Len Kachinsky. *Making a Murderer* revealed that, shortly after being appointed to the case but before meeting with his client, Kachinsky told the media that Dassey was "morally and legally responsible" for the part he played in the Halbach murder.[11] In addition to this public statement, Kachinsky also sent a private investigator, Michael O'Kelly, to interrogate Dassey for the purpose of obtaining his own client's confession. In so doing, O'Kelly employed interrogation tactics that were so coercive they probably would have made Mark Wiegert and Tom Fassbender blush.

O'Kelly also lied to Dassey by telling him that he (Dassey) had failed his lie detector test, when in fact he hadn't.[12] He told Dassey that continuing to assert his innocence meant that he was continuing to lie. He told Dassey that, in order to help him, Dassey must select from one of two choices on a form: (1) "I am very sorry for what I did" or (2) "I am *not* sorry for what I did."[13] (Nowhere was innocence offered as a choice.) He even made Dassey draw a picture of the bloody rape, throat slashing, and murder—the details of which Dassey dreamed up during his previous interrogations with Wiegert and Fassbender. Kachinsky and O'Kelly then offered their client's statements and drawings to the government, and also invited Wiegert and Fassbender to again interrogate Dassey, without Kachinsky being present.

Kachinsky's strategy in doing all of this was to firm up Dassey's earlier confession to Wiegert and Fassbender, to fully cooperate with the government's prosecution of Avery (even though such cooperation also incriminated Dassey), and to have Dassey testify against Avery at Avery's trial. In return, Kachinsky was hoping to receive a plea bargain for Dassey from the state.[14]

Dassey's appellate lawyers, however, argued that Kachinsky's performance was deficient in numerous ways. They argued that Kachinsky should not have publicly admitted his client's guilt without first meeting with him and exploring the numerous possible defenses available to him—defenses that may have included the coercion defense, an alibi defense, and a false confession defense, among others.

Dassey's appellate lawyers argued that Kachinsky should not have made the strategic decision to cooperate with the government without first receiving a plea offer from the prosecutor, and then presenting it to, and discussing it with, his client. They also argued that, in the face of his client's continued claims of innocence, Kachinsky should not have continued down the strategic path he had chosen.

Dassey's appellate lawyers further argued that Kachinsky should not have employed O'Kelly to lie to and interrogate his own client for the purpose of obtaining a confession to turn over to the state. They also argued that Kachinsky should not have invited government agents to again interrogate his client—without Kachinsky being present, no less.

In support of their argument that Kachinsky's performance was deficient—that is, he failed to satisfy the standards of loyalty, diligence, and competence, and failed to communicate with his client and keep his client's confidences—the appellate lawyers used the trial judge's own words to Dassey's advantage. When Kachinsky was allowed to withdraw as counsel before Dassey's trial started, the trial judge said Kachinsky's "failure to be present while his client gave a statement to investigators . . . I believe that constituted *deficient performance* on Attorney Kachinsky's part. . . . This is not the kind of assistance of counsel a defendant should have."[15]

Having made a case—and, given the trial judge's words, a seemingly strong case—for deficient performance, Dassey's appellate lawyers then moved on to the prejudice prong of the two-part test. They argued that not only did Kachinsky perform deficiently, but Dassey was prejudiced by that deficiency. Specifically, they once again relied on the trial judge's own words. When Dassey talked to the government interrogators—at Kachinsky's invitation and without Kachinsky being present—the government obtained yet another statement from Dassey that it was able to use to its advantage. The trial judge called it "a statement which, according to the special prosecutor's petition filed May 17 supporting his motion to increase bail[,] provided *new information to authorities on the crimes charged* here. . . ."[16]

Most harmful of all, when interrogating Dassey without Kachinsky present, Wiegert and Fassbender told the simplistic, overmatched teenager that he had better admit some of his transgressions to his mother. If he didn't, then *they* would tell her that he had been lying to them again. Dassey promised to talk to his mother when she came to visit, but that was not good enough for the wily interrogators. They wanted him to call his mother and discuss it on the phone.

Why was it so important to the government that Dassey call his mother on the phone? Because the government was recording all of Dassey's jail phone calls. And Dassey's statements made during phone calls with his mother would appear, to a jury, to be far removed from the coercive pressure of the interrogation room. This, of course, would be a better quality of evidence for the state to use at trial. Wiegert therefore insisted to Dassey, "[I]t would be a good idea to call [your mom] and tell her before she gets here tonight. That's what I would do. Cuz, otherwise, she's gonna be really mad. . . . *Better on the phone,* isn't it?"[17]

"Better on the phone," indeed. Better for the government, that is. Dassey called his mother, discussed the case, and his recorded phone call was used against him at his own trial where he was convicted as a "party to" the murder of Teresa Halbach.

A NEW TRIAL?

Let's revisit some of the ethics rules from earlier. Was Kachinsky loyal to Dassey or did he seem to be working more for the state in its pursuit of Steven Avery? Did he diligently explore possible defenses for Dassey before telling the media that his client was "morally and legally responsible"? Did he competently represent Dassey when he invited Wiegert and Fassbender to interrogate him again—without even attending the interrogation to keep an eye out for Dassey's interests? And did he effectively communicate with Dassey about important matters and keep Dassey's confidences? To put it in terms of the two-part, ineffective assistance of counsel test, did Kachinsky perform deficiently, and, if so, was Dassey prejudiced by that deficient performance?

After reading chapter 2, no one should be surprised that the conviction-affirming appellate court denied Dassey's request for a new trial. The appellate court, with virtually no analysis whatsoever, swiftly dispensed with Dassey's claim of ineffective assistance of counsel via six superficial paragraphs. In these paragraphs it simply ignored the vast majority of the appellate lawyers' evidence and arguments. Instead, the appellate court first concluded that Kachinsky's actions were reasonable, in that "he hoped to get the best deal he could for Dassey. . . ."[18] The court then held that, even though the state used Dassey's phone calls against him at trial, the appellate lawyers failed to demonstrate a "viable link between Kachinsky's actions and any demonstrable detriment" to Dassey.[19]

To put this in baseball terms, Dassey's appellate lawyers needed to connect on both pitches. They needed to hit the ball out of the park on both issues—deficient performance *and* prejudice—in order to get Dassey a new trial. And although they seemed to have launched both pitches deep into the cheap seats, the appellate court simply dismissed their work as nothing more than two foul balls. And in this game, it's two strikes and you're out. The state appellate court affirmed Dassey's conviction.[20]

PROTECTING CLIENTS FROM ATTORNEYS

It is important to remember that the Office of Lawyer Regulation (OLR) and the Wisconsin State Bar never found that Kachinsky violated any ethics rule. (Nor, to my knowledge, was there even an allegation that he did so.) Further, contrary to the trial judge's initial statement that Kachinsky's performance was "not the kind of assistance of counsel a defendant should have," the appellate court held that Kachinsky satisfied the attorney performance standards and rendered effective assistance of counsel.[21]

The problem, therefore, to the extent that one even exists, is with "the system." And the questions are these. With regard to criminal defense lawyers, do we really even value the principles of loyalty, diligence, competence, communication, and confidentiality? If not, then fine. But if we do, are we satisfied with a system where Kachinsky's performance in Dassey's case is deemed to have satisfied these standards? If we are not satisfied, then our entire system—the disastrous ethics rules, the malleable attorney performance standards, and the flaccid appellate court judges—needs to be revamped from the ground up. (Keep in mind, however, that a new, more robust system would protect *all* criminal defendants—not just those who are featured in popular documentaries and widely perceived to be innocent.)

But until we get this new, more robust system, how will the OLR and the Wisconsin State Bar justify their continued bureaucratic existence? As discussed in chapter 11, they still have plenty of ways to pretend they are serving the public. And, as discussed in the next chapter, if things get really slow, they can always spend their time ferreting out and disciplining attorneys who have an "offensive personality."[22] However, while doling out such discipline will perpetuate the illusion that the OLR and the Wisconsin State Bar are protecting clients from their lawyers,[23] it won't help Avery, Dassey, or any other defendant accused of a crime.

Chapter 13
THE MINISTER OF JUSTICE

"He wasn't seeking the truth, he was seeking a conviction."
—Pete Baetz, investigator, on prosecutor Ken Kratz

W isconsin's criminal code is, to put it mildly, out of control. The crimes are countless—literally.[1] And the criminal penalties are enormous. Additionally, as explained in chapter 9, prosecutors can stack charges on top of each other so that a defendant is essentially facing a life sentence, even when he is accused of only a single criminal incident and even when no person was harmed in any serious way. And in cases like Avery's, stacking just two charges is enough for a prosecutor to win a split verdict—in effect, a conviction and life sentence without juror unanimity.

Because prosecutors have such tremendous, life-ruining power, Wisconsin's ethics rules impose additional burdens on them. Broadly speaking, this begins with the recognition that the "prosecutor has the responsibility of a minister of justice and not simply that of an advocate. This responsibility carries with it specific obligations to see that the defendant is accorded procedural justice and that guilt is decided upon the basis of sufficient evidence."[2]

Ensuring such procedural justice is especially important in cases with extensive pretrial publicity. Here, the rules are more specific than merely anointing the prosecutor with a vague but noble-sounding title. In general, a prosecutor is not permitted to make public statements that would prejudice a defendant. More specifically, a prosecutor may not make pretrial, public statements about (1) "the character, credibility, reputation or criminal record" of the defendant; (2) "the existence or contents of any confession, admission, or statement given by a defendant or suspect"; and (3) the prosecutor's personal "opinion as to the guilt or innocence of a defendant or suspect in a criminal case. . . ."[3]

And the prosecutor's duty includes ensuring that others in the government shut their mouths as well. The prosecutor must "exercise reasonable care to prevent investigators, law enforcement personnel, employees or other persons assisting or associated with the prosecutor in a criminal case from making an extrajudicial statement that the prosecutor would be prohibited from making. . . ."[4]

PRETRIAL PUBLICITY IN *MAKING A MURDERER*

Let's take a look at how effective the ethics rules on pretrial publicity were in protecting Avery's and Dassey's right to a fair trial, including their right to procedural justice and their right to be tried on the evidence in court rather than in the media.

Special prosecutor Ken Kratz and Calumet County sheriff Jerry Pagel each held numerous press conferences and gave several televised interviews about the Teresa Halbach murder. Often, the two of them sat right next to each other when doing so.[5] And again, for purposes of the ethics rules, Pagel's statements would be attributable to Kratz, as Kratz has the responsibility to control those government agents assisting him or associated with him in the criminal case.

Here are some of the things the two of them said during their media tour. Contrary to the rule that appears to prohibit disclosure of "the existence or contents" of a suspect's statement or confession, Pagel, while sitting right next to Kratz, announced that Dassey was "taken into custody" because he "admitted his involvement in the death of Teresa Halbach as well as Steven Avery's involvement in this matter."[6]

Soon thereafter, Kratz got more specific about Dassey's alleged confession. With his inner novelist breaking free, he painted a vivid picture for the media:

> As Brendan approaches the trailer . . . Brendan already starts to hear the screams. . . . He knocks on Steven Avery's trailer door. . . .

[He] has to wait, until the person he knows as his uncle, who is partially dressed, who is full of sweat, opens the door and greets his sixteen year old nephew. . . . Teresa Halbach is begging Brendan for her life. . . . Steven Avery at this point invites his sixteen year old nephew to sexually assault this woman he has bound to the bed. During the rape, Teresa is begging for help. . . .[7]

The media, of course, made no inquiry into the reliability of Dassey's alleged statement or the circumstances under which it was obtained. Instead, the media presented it in even more dramatic fashion to viewers, some of whom were interviewed and expressed their disgust and their opinions that the two defendants were, of course, guilty. After all, if it's on a local Wisconsin news channel, then it must be true.

This fiasco proves the utter uselessness of the ethics rule that (supposedly) prohibits a lawyer from disclosing "the existence or contents of any confession, admission, or statement given by a defendant or suspect." The rule might as well have never been written.

But what about the ethics rule prohibiting statements about "the character, credibility, reputation or criminal record" of the defendant? Here, Manitowoc County sheriff Ken Petersen took over. On Petersen's leg of the government's media tour, he gave a televised interview and said he "knows the Averys" and is also aware of "Steven's colorful past." He said that, if released, Avery would kill again, because "I think that's his personality." He also insisted that the Manitowoc Sheriff's Department did not frame Avery, because it would have been easier simply to kill him. "If, if we wanted him out of the picture, like in prison, or if we wanted him, um, killed, ya know, it would have been much easier just to kill him."[8]

These are stunning statements from an elected public official in law *enforcement*. Dean Strang said it simply, but best: "This is absolutely insane."[9] But at least the people of Manitowoc, Wisconsin, can rest easy knowing that their elected sheriff has considered, and weighed the relative difficulties, both of framing and killing one of the town's citizens.

Finally, what about the ethics rule that a prosecutor may not give his "opinion as to the guilt or innocence of a defendant or suspect in a criminal case"? Here, Ken Kratz stepped back onto center stage. Early in the case, he recounted for the media all of the evidence against Avery, and concluded, "It is no longer a question, at least in my mind as the special prosecutor in this case, who is responsible for the death of Teresa Halbach."[10]

Telling the media that, "in [his] mind," Avery is guilty of killing Halbach seems to be the very definition of giving an "opinion as to the guilt . . . of a defendant." Once again, the rule isn't worth the paper (or web page) on which it is printed.

The point is not that Kratz violated an ethics rule; rather, to my knowledge he was never found to have violated any ethics rule during the course of prosecuting Avery and Dassey. In fact, this issue of pretrial publicity was litigated, and Kratz found legal shelter in the numerous exceptions to the rules. More specifically, Kratz painted his and law enforcement's multiple, lengthy press conferences as ethically permissible responses to Avery's statements to the media. Kratz wrote,

> [P]rior to (and after) November 11, 2005, Steven Avery, family members, supporters, and other citizens advanced the theory that Avery was being "set up" by law enforcement officials, and the court will note that information disseminated [in the government's press conferences] specifically refuted [Avery's] conspiracy theory as authorized by SCR 20:3.6 (d).[11]

Was Kratz's reliance on this exception justified? The answer depends on whether "a reasonable lawyer would believe" that the prosecutor's and law enforcement's media interviews were "required to protect [the state] from the substantial likelihood of undue prejudicial effect" caused by Avery's statements.[12]

A strong argument can certainly be made that Kratz's, Pagel's, and Petersen's statements were *not* "required" in order to protect the state. For example, when a defendant says that he has been framed by the cops, is it really "required" for a sheriff to talk about the defendant's "colorful past" or his "personality"? And is it really "required" for a prosecutor to express his own personal opinion about the defendant's guilt? And, regardless of what a defendant says to the media, is it ever "required" for a sheriff to talk about the relative difficulties of both framing and killing him? A strong argument can indeed be made that the government's media blitz, allegedly done for the purpose of "refut[ing] Avery's conspiracy theory," was the equivalent of using a giant sledgehammer to kill a mosquito sitting on a glass coffee table.

But even if a reasonable lawyer would believe that the government's multiple, televised press conferences were "required to protect [the state]" from Avery's claims of innocence, what about *Dassey's* right to be tried in court and not in the media? After all, it was Dassey's alleged confession that Ken Kratz was recounting in lurid detail and dramatic effect, even though Dassey never said a word to the media and never accused any government agency of framing him.

Just asking these questions proves the point that when clients really need the ethics rules, the rules fail miserably. When it comes to these important situations, the rules are hyper-nuanced, ultra-flexible gibberish—the word "reasonable" even rears its ugly head once again—and do absolutely nothing to protect the very people they were supposedly designed to protect.

Although, in fairness, Avery did not help himself; he seemed to talk at every opportunity. For example, when this now thirty-year-old saga began, his statements at the time of his arrest in the Beerntsen case were used against him at trial and in his appeal.[13] In the Halbach case, he again talked to law enforcement—both before and after his arrest—and some of those statements were used against him at trial.[14] Then, as discussed above, his post-charging statements in the Halbach case launched the government's better organized, more effective, and much more widely disseminated anti-Avery media campaign. And due in large part to the numerous, televised press conferences starring Ken Kratz, Jerry Pagel, Ken Petersen, and others, Avery's jury pool was so infected that 129 out of 130 potential jurors stated in their juror questionnaires that Avery was probably guilty. In numerous ways, Avery has proven that, for criminal defendants, pre-trial silence can be golden.

SOPHISTRY AND THE MINISTER OF JUSTICE

The Sophists of ancient Greece were not well liked:

> The Sophists' reputation . . . suffered because of their emphasis on winning debates in and out of court at all costs. Since they believed that power was the ultimate value, the key issue became not right or wrong, but getting your own way. . . . As the Sophists became expert debaters and advertisers, they learned to use emotional appeals, physical appearance, and clever language to sell their particular point of view. These characteristics have led to the modern meaning of "a sophistry" as an example of overly subtle, superficially plausible, but *ultimately fallacious reasoning.*[15]

Upon reading the above account, most people would associate sophistry with criminal defense lawyers, not prosecutors. And, in theory, that would make sense. A defense lawyer, after all, works only for his client, whereas the prosecutor works for his client (the state) *and* is supposed to be a minister of justice. Therefore, a prosecutor should never resort to "physical appearance," "emotional appeals," or "clever language" to win a case.

But let's take a closer look at Ken Kratz's performance in *Making a Murderer.* First, the footage in the documentary did demonstrate that Kratz took care to dress well, keep the hair on his head combed, and keep his mustache in good order. He also, without question, appealed to the public's and the jurors' emotions. This, of course, was easy to do, given that a young woman had been murdered and incinerated.

But do these things alone a Sophist make? Let's get more specific and look at some of Kratz's "clever language" in his closing argument to the jury. First, Jerry Buting and Dean Strang maintained, from the very beginning, that someone else killed Halbach and then brought her car and her body to the Avery property. The defense even made clear that the sheriffs had nothing to do with Halbach's death. Rather, when the sheriffs saw the evidence that appeared to link Avery to the crime, they firmly (but wrongly) believed Avery was guilty. Based on this erroneous belief, they took steps to frame a supposedly guilty man. Despite this, Kratz still argued to the jury that, to buy into Avery's defense, the jurors would have to believe the cops were the murderers:

> The cops had to kill her. Are you as the jury, in order to find Mr. Avery not guilty, willing to say that your cops, that your Manitowoc County Sheriff's Deputies, Lieutenant Lenk and Sergeant Colborn came across a twenty-five-year-old photographer, killed her, mutilated her, burned her bones, all to set up and to frame Mr. Avery? You gotta be willing to say that! You gotta make that leap![16]

But this argument might not qualify as sophistry: it was not "overly subtle" or even "superficially plausible." Again, the defense never asserted that the Manitowoc sheriffs would even be capable of killing Halbach (despite Sheriff Ken Petersen's own musings that it would be easier to kill than to frame a person). Rather, Kratz's argument was simply a flat-out bad argument. It was really just a gross mischaracterization of Avery's defense, and probably appealed only to jurors who had already convicted Avery in their minds. Any open-minded juror who had yet to form an opinion on the case should have seen straight through this prosecutorial gibberish—and should have been insulted by it.

But more alarming than this, and definitely qualifying as sophistry, was Kratz's argument to the jury that "reasonable doubts are for innocent people."[17] This argument was subtle, had some superficial appeal to it, but was definitely a misstatement of the burden of proof. That is, Kratz was urging the jurors to do the exact opposite of what they should do.

The jury is legally obligated to start with the presumption of innocence, evaluate the evidence for reasonable doubt, and *then* render a verdict. Kratz, on the other hand, was urging the jury to do the reverse. He urged the jury to first conclude—whether based on emotion, gut feeling, or speculation—that Avery was guilty. Then, because Avery was guilty, Kratz urged the jurors to disregard their reasonable doubts about the evidence. Why? Because "reasonable doubts are for *innocent* people," not guilty people like Avery. In Kratz's argument, it is Avery's guilt that dispenses with the need to evaluate the evidence for reasonable doubt.

This argument was subtle and superficially appealing. It may have even appealed to jurors who, to that point, had maintained an open mind about the case. And unfortunately, the court did nothing to debunk Kratz's sophistry. Rather, as discussed in chapter 7, the court instructed the jury "not to search for doubt," but instead "to search for the truth."[18] This erroneous, harmful, and unconstitutional language is somewhat similar (in an odd, twisted way) to Kratz's argument. That is, if it is true that Avery is guilty, then the jury should not search for doubt.

THE IRONY OF THE ETHICS RULES

Earlier I stated that Ken Kratz (and Len Kachinsky) did not violate any ethics rules in the Avery and Dassey cases. Alternatively, one could argue that Kratz *did* violate the ethics rules by disclosing the content of Dassey's alleged confession, by not properly controlling the sheriff's department's statements about Avery, by expressing his own personal beliefs about Avery's guilt, and by making arguments to the jury that conflicted with his duties as a minister of justice. I, however, do *not* make such a leap. Rather, I contend that the ethics rules—with all of their exceptions, nuances, subtleties, vagaries, and multiple interpretations—are to blame. These rules—rules that can be far too draconian for no reason whatsoever, and far too lax on matters that are really important—are an absolute disaster. And it is this disaster that failed Avery and Dassey, and continues to fail defendants in Wisconsin and every other state that adopted the American Bar Association's Model Rules of Professional Conduct.

Ironically, though, Ken Kratz was disciplined for an ethics violation, but it had nothing to do with his prosecution of Avery and Dassey. Instead, as shown near the end of *Making a Murderer*, Kratz sent several text messages to an alleged victim in a domestic violence case that he was prosecuting. In the messages, Kratz was pursuing a relationship of some sort: "You maybe [sic] the tall, young, hot nymph, but I am the prize." Kratz is also alleged to have made inappropriate comments—including comments about the breast size he prefers in his women—in front of others and during the course of his prosecutorial duties. As a result of these text messages and comments, Kratz was disciplined for having an "offensive personality" in violation of the ethics rules.[19]

In this book I have been critical of "the system," and have not condemned any individual lawyer, including Len Kachinsky and Ken Kratz—two lawyers who have received much negative attention since *Making a Murderer* was released. However, I will concede that Kratz's text messages and discussion of breast size in the workplace strike me as inappropriate. Yet, these ethics violations certainly played no role in convicting anyone of murder. But despite the relatively low impact that Kratz's "offensive personality" had on the world at large, Kratz had his law license suspended for four months and had to pay $23,904.10 for the cost of the disciplinary proceedings against him.[20]

Even assuming that Kratz's rule violations for "offensive personality" warranted a four-month license suspension, I challenge anyone to explain how the cost of the ethics investigation—an investigation into Kratz's text messages and verbal statements—could have possibly totaled $23,904.10. In fact, there wasn't even a disciplinary hearing to pay for; rather, Kratz waived it by pleading no contest to several of the allegations.

Kratz himself offers an explanation for the staggering cost. In some ways his comments echo my own criticism of the Office of Lawyer Regulation (OLR) and the Wisconsin State Bar set forth in chapter 11. I argued that these bureaucracies create the apparent self-serving illusion that they are protecting the public from the lawyers. And, with regard to his own ethics investigation, Kratz argued that "he wanted to settle the case [even earlier] in the disciplinary process, but the OLR refused to do so, in part because [the OLR] is apparently more concerned with how they look in the zealous pursuit of an attorney pelt, rather than what result should be reached."[21]

Kratz's remarks about the OLR's concern with "how they look" politically, and their "zealous pursuit" of him for symbolic purposes, are somewhat ironic given Kratz's zealous pursuit of Avery and Dassey. Nonetheless, Kratz's comments about the bureaucracy ring true. And his comments also lead nicely into our next chapter.

Chapter 14

THE POLITICS OF LEGAL REFORM

"You can't put people in prison because you think someday they might do something wrong. . . . But you still have these conflicting thoughts and feelings."

—Rep. Mark Gundrum

Sometimes, meaningful legal reform is incredibly simple. For example, chapter 7 discussed Wisconsin's burden of proof requirement for criminal trials. The judge in Steven Avery's trial for the murder of Teresa Halbach used the statewide pattern jury instruction that defines the phrase "reasonable doubt," but then concludes by telling the jury "*not* to search for doubt," but instead "to search for the *truth*."[1] The chapter then went on to demonstrate, both logically and empirically, how this instruction actually lowered the state's burden of proof below the constitutionally mandated "beyond a reasonable doubt" standard.

Lowering the state's burden of proof is an incredibly serious problem—in theory, it could be the most serious problem discussed in this entire book. However, the solution is as simple as fixing the last two lines of Wisconsin's standard jury instruction. The truth-related language should be removed, and the instruction should simply conclude as follows: "It is your duty to give the defendant the benefit of every reasonable doubt."[2] If the jury instruction were to be changed and made mandatory, it would be difficult (although not impossible) for prosecutors and judges to worm their way around this constitutionally mandated burden of proof.

With other legal issues, however, substantive reform can be next to meaningless. For example, we saw in chapter 4 that at the time of Avery's trial Wisconsin courts had an anything-goes approach to expert testimony. The result was that a prosecutor could call a government employee with a PhD to testify as an expert, even though the witness was nothing more than the state's advocate wearing a scientist's clothing. This allowed the prosecutor to put the gloss of expert witness testimony on the case, and it increased his chances of winning a conviction.

Since that time, however, Wisconsin switched to the Daubert standard, which, in theory, is a much tougher standard and only permits *reliable* expert testimony to reach the jury's ears. But the problem, as we saw, is that the Daubert standard allows trial judges to use ten or more factors—in their discretion and in any manner they wish—to determine what counts as reliable. Because too much discretion was placed in the hands of trial judges, it's as if the well-intentioned legal reform never happened. Trial judges, and the appellate judges who uphold their rulings, have completely circumvented the new law.

This chapter will now offer two specific recommendations. Each of the next two sections will briefly revisit a legal issue of national significance from *Making a Murderer*. Each section will then set forth a specific legal reform proposal to address the problem. The legal issues, which by this point will be familiar, are (1) the judiciary's near-absolute ban of the wrong-person defense, and (2) law enforcement's tactics for evading Miranda, which, in turn, can lead to false confessions.

The recommendations for reform are complex—at least relative to much of the discussion in earlier chapters. But as you read the next two sections, think of how effective the proposed legal reform would be when placed in the hands of pro-state trial or appellate judges. Would the new law be clear-cut and therefore difficult to evade, like the proposed change in the burden of proof jury instruction? Or would the new law be mere putty in the hands of a judge hellbent on ensuring (or affirming) the defendant's conviction, much like the Daubert reform for expert witness testimony? Or would the new law fall somewhere in between these two extremes? It is difficult to predict; often, a reform that initially looks promising ends up easily circumvented by the very government agents the reform was intended to constrain.

THE WRONG-PERSON DEFENSE

Chapter 5 discussed how, in both of his cases, Avery was prevented from using a third-party defense at trial. That is, Avery's defense teams were not permitted to tell the juries who they believed committed the crimes with which Avery was charged. The chapter went on to explain how Wisconsin courts, along with many other state courts, have created an irrational double standard that actually hides evidence of innocence from the jury. More specifically, before a defendant may argue that a third party committed the crime, the Denny rule requires that he provide the court with (1) the third party's motive for committing the crime; (2) evidence of the third party's opportunity to commit the crime; and (3) direct evidence linking the third party to the crime.

Because it is nearly impossible for a defendant to satisfy this three-part Denny test, I recommended significant legal reform in my article "An Alternative to the Wrong-Person Defense," originally published in volume 24 (pp. 1–37) of the *George Mason University Civil Rights Law Journal* in 2013. The portion of the article dealing with the recommended legal reform is reproduced below. (Internal citations and footnotes in the original article have been omitted.)

> The necessary reform in the law of the wrong-person defense is simple. . . . Reform begins by abolishing the three-part test for admissibility in jurisdictions in which it is used. There is simply no justification for courts to insist a defendant must provide direct rather than circumstantial evidence of third-party guilt, while at the same time instructing the jury that, with regard to the prosecutor's case, circumstantial evidence is just as good as direct evidence. Further, there is no reason for courts to require a defendant to prove the third party's motive to commit the crime, when the jury is instructed that the prosecutor is not required to prove the defendant's motive.
>
> Instead, the test for admissibility should be the same as that for any other line of evidence: relevance. Further, the test must not determine whether a court believes the defendant's wrong-person defense *as a whole* is relevant. Under this type of analysis, trial judges

inevitably confuse the weight of the evidence with its admissibility and often exclude the defense because, in their opinion, it is not strong enough. Rather, the relevancy test must apply to each piece of the defendant's evidence *individually*.

For example, if the defendant is aware of a third party's motive to commit the crime, even without being able to prove opportunity or to provide direct evidence of third-party guilt, that motive evidence is always relevant. Similarly, if the defendant can show that a third party had the opportunity to commit the crime, even without an apparent motive or direct evidence of guilt, that opportunity evidence is always relevant. Further, if the defendant can produce circumstantial evidence of third-party guilt or evidence of the third party's consciousness of guilt, even without direct evidence, that circumstantial evidence is always relevant. Any one of these pieces of evidence is always relevant and would be sufficient to convict the defendant if the prosecution offered such evidence against him. Therefore, this same type of evidence should be admissible against the prosecution in an attempt to raise reasonable doubt concerning the defendant's guilt.

Second, courts should not require a defendant to divulge his wrong-person defense before trial through pretrial offers of proof or motions to admit evidence, just as courts do not require the government to divulge its theory of the case before trial.

Third, courts should never exclude a wrong-person defense based on the possibility that it could confuse the jury. Excluding third-party guilt evidence because of jury confusion or similar pretextual reasons is currently a common judicial tactic, even in states and federal courts that do not explicitly apply the stringent, three-part test for admissibility. However, because creating reasonable doubt about the defendant's guilt is the legitimate purpose of all defense evidence—and, further, because a truly speculative wrong-person defense will only make the government's case look stronger—the wrong-person defense creates no risk of an erroneous acquittal.

Finally, courts should not impose new, additional hurdles for the defendant to leap, such as proving the third party did not have an alibi or proving the precise number of perpetrators involved in the crime. Similarly, courts also should not elevate the rules of evidence, even when accurately applied, above the defendant's constitutional right to present a defense.

Although these recommendations are both straightforward and desperately needed, the undeniable reality is that proposals for legal reform are typically of little or no value. Even the most logical proposals to change the most obvious problems may simply be ignored by the state supreme courts and the Supreme Court of the United States. Further, in the rare cases where courts do attempt legal reform, they often wait many decades after a constitutional problem has been identified. Even then, courts typically lack the fortitude and the practical knowledge necessary to truly constrain prosecutorial and judicial abuses of individual rights.[3]

MIRANDA, INTERROGATIONS, AND FALSE CONFESSIONS

An issue closely related to false confessions is whether the suspect was adequately informed of his Miranda rights before he began speaking to police. For example, chapter 6 discussed how the cops interrogated Brendan Dassey multiple times without reading him his Miranda rights. Then, once they did read him his rights, Dassey promptly waived them and talked. He then confessed to, and was tried and convicted for, an incredibly bloody crime of rape, torture, and murder. However, the crime, as Dassey tells it, is contradicted by all of the physical evidence and appears never to have happened. And other than his bizarre confession, there was no other evidence linking him to Halbach's death.

Of course, if the Miranda warnings had adequately protected Dassey, he never would have falsely confessed because he never would have talked to the cops in the first place. In response to the problem of Miranda abuses, Anthony Domanico, Lawrence White, and I studied actual recorded police interrogations from Wisconsin, and recommended Miranda reforms in our article "Overcoming Miranda: A Content Analysis of the Miranda Portion of Police Interrogations," originally published in volume 49 (pp. 1–22) of the *Idaho Law Review* in 2012. The portion of the article dealing with our recommended legal reforms is reproduced below. (Internal citations and footnotes in the original article have been omitted.)

Our findings, combined with those of other social scientists, support specific reforms that would advance the Court's stated policy of protecting individual rights by ensuring that [*Miranda*] waivers are truly made "voluntarily, knowingly, and intelligently."

First, the police should be required to electronically record all custodial interrogations. A permanent and accurate record of the *Miranda* portion of police interrogations is virtually a prerequisite to determining whether a suspect has made a voluntary, knowing, and intelligent waiver of his rights. Without such a recording, courts will have "difficulty in depicting what transpires at such interrogations" and will instead rely exclusively on after-the-fact police testimony about the event. This means, of course, that virtually every *Miranda* waiver will be held to be legally valid, regardless of what actually took place in the secretive "incommunicado interrogation."

Second, the police should be prohibited from minimizing the importance of the Miranda warning. Minimization tactics were employed in nearly half of the interrogations in our sample, and were likely a substantial reason the police were able to obtain waivers in more than 90% of all interrogations in the sample. Minimization techniques are, by their very nature, clearly at direct odds with a suspect having "full awareness of both the nature of the right[s] being abandoned and the consequences of the decision to abandon [them]."

Preventing minimization techniques could be accomplished in at least two ways: first, trial courts could be required to rule that minimization techniques render a waiver involuntary, much the way that threats or promises render a waiver (or even the subsequent statement itself) involuntary; and second, the Miranda warning could include specific language that emphasizes the importance of the underlying rights.

Third, the presentation of the Miranda warnings should be modified to make them understandable to all or most suspects. The Miranda warnings that were used as the basis for this study required, overall, a tenth-grade reading level, while most criminal suspects fall well below that. Further, and even more alarming, the last two warnings used in our study—the right to a free attorney and the right to stop answering questions after the suspect initially waives the right to remain silent—required reading levels of 13.0 and 18.7, respectively, thus rendering them incomprehensible to most criminal suspects and even to many college students.

In addition to (or in lieu of) modifying the language of the warning itself, three modifications to the presentation of the warning—instructing the suspect as to the nature of the upcoming information, listing and presenting each right separately, and explaining each right in a slightly different manner—have been shown to improve comprehension dramatically. These modifications improve the "listenability" of the warning because: (a) suspects know what to listen for and can focus their attention on the task at hand; (b) the information is separated into discrete packets, which introduces a helpful pause between each of the Miranda rights and eases the burden on working (short-term) memory; and (c) built-in redundancies allow suspects to capture any information they may have missed the first time. In one study, adding all three modifications to a standard warning nearly doubled the average comprehension score.

Fourth, the police should be required to present the warning both orally and in written form. This practice would enhance understanding for many suspects because statements that are difficult to comprehend are more easily understood when presented in written form as opposed to orally. Indeed, one experiment found that pretrial defendants were much less likely to understand their Miranda rights when the rights were read orally instead of presented in written form. The extra time devoted to administration of Miranda would also allow suspects to consider more carefully their rights and whether they wish to waive those rights.

Fifth, the police should be required to actively assess the degree to which suspects understand their rights. This can be easily accomplished by asking suspects to paraphrase Miranda rights in their own words, as two of the interrogators did in our sample. Police should also be required to clarify any misconceptions or misunderstandings that the suspect may have.

If police departments adopt a paraphrasing protocol, suspects should be asked to paraphrase each element separately. Any attempt to paraphrase the content of the Miranda warnings in their entirety would overwhelm the cognitive resources of most suspects. A model warning that incorporates a paraphrasing protocol—and that can be understood by individuals who read at a second-grade level—is readily available. When police test a suspect's understanding of his or her rights, attorneys and judges can be more confident that a knowing and intelligent Miranda waiver was obtained by the police.

Sixth and finally, the police should be required to obtain written acknowledgement that the suspect understands each right. Such acknowledgement must occur immediately after each right is presented. This practice would prevent police from presenting the rights in a rapid and uninterrupted torrent, with no pauses between separate elements.

Some might argue that these safeguards are unnecessary when a suspect has a lengthy arrest record; indeed, even the U.S. Supreme Court has embraced the notion that repeated Miranda advisements lead to better comprehension and recall. Empirical research, however, fails to support this contention. "Frequent flyers" who have been arrested more than 20 times do not differ appreciably from less-experienced defendants in their ability to comprehend and recall Miranda warnings.[4]

SPITTING IN THE WIND

The above-described legal reforms—modifying Wisconsin's burden of proof jury instruction, eliminating the Denny rule on third-party guilt evidence, and strengthening suspects' Miranda safeguards—may never be implemented. Substantive legal reform rarely happens because it is the rational or right thing to do. Rather, it usually happens when lawmakers are motivated to ride the emotional wave of a single, high-profile injustice that has captured the public's attention. And that is exactly what happened when Avery was released from prison eighteen years after his wrongful conviction for the Beerntsen rape. This highly publicized event led to the Avery bill, the Avery Commission, the Avery Task Force, and other similarly named, politically popular reform activities. Politicians were even lined up for photo ops with Avery—all in the name of justice, but with the obvious intention of advancing their careers.

But then this legal reform momentum came to a screeching halt when the Manitowoc Sheriff's Department again arrested Avery, this time for the Teresa Halbach murder. Instead of maintaining an open mind, people immediately gave the benefit of the doubt to the sheriffs—the same law enforcement agency that already proved its institutional incompetence in Avery's first case—and rushed, once again, to declare Avery's guilt.

In *Making a Murderer*, Wisconsin representative Mark Gundrum commented, "As much as you mentally want to give the benefit of the doubt to [Avery], it becomes impossible."[5] (It would seem more appropriate to direct such skepticism toward the Manitowoc Sheriff's Department.) He further mused, "And then ya start thinkin' ta yourself, boy, maybe it was good [Avery] was in all that time, as unjust as it was. If he did this, what might he have done during that time?"[6] (Interestingly, this fails to account for the additional women *actually* victimized by Gregory Allen, the real perpetrator, because Avery, rather than Allen, was sitting in jail.)

And the media was no better. Its rush to judgment was so swift that it even raised political chatter of instituting the death penalty in Wisconsin—long before Avery was even convicted. And many members of the community, having already tried and convicted Avery in their minds, jumped on the media's brain-dead bandwagon and flooded Avery's family members with incredibly threatening and intimidating letters.

Further, after the conviction, the Wisconsin courts would do nothing to assist Avery and Dassey, even knowing what the law enforcement agents had done to Avery in the Beerntsen case. Dassey's appellate lawyer Steven Drizin fully recognized the political nature of criminal justice in Wisconsin: "It would be very difficult for Brendan to get relief in the Wisconsin state court system. This case was just too much of a heater."[7]

However, *Making a Murderer* has, without question, helped regain some of the legal reform momentum that was lost the very second Avery was even suspected of murdering Teresa Halbach. But for Avery, at least, more is probably needed. As his lawyers speculated near the end of the documentary, it will likely take some newly discovered, incredibly powerful, and near-conclusive evidence to turn the tide—not only for Avery, but for the Wisconsin legal reform movement generally.

But even if Avery's case stalls, it's only a matter of time before the next Wisconsin prisoner—one who has been locked up for twenty years, thirty years, or even longer—is exonerated. And depending on whether that defendant is politically marketable, such an exoneration could recapture the public's attention and put criminal law reform back in the spotlight. In other words, Wisconsin needs the next Steven Avery.

Until then, legal reform initiatives will likely continue to favor the government, rather than our individual rights and freedoms. As a criminal defense lawyer and a member of the Wisconsin Association of Criminal Defense Lawyers, I frequently receive legislative updates for the state of Wisconsin. And it seems that, on a frequent basis, criminal penalties are being increased, new criminal laws are being added, and defendants' procedural rights are being eroded.

One recent legislative reform sticks in my memory as an example of a pure political play. Currently, it is a felony in Wisconsin to spit on an emergency medical technician, a first responder, a law enforcement officer, a fire fighter, or a person operating or staffing an ambulance.[8] Now, thanks to Act 340 (passed as Assembly Bill 357), Wisconsin has added "district attorney," "deputy district attorney," and "assistant district attorney" to the list of persons protected from saliva.[9]

But what about other prosecutors who don't have one of those three titles? What about "special prosecutors" who, like Ken Kratz, are brought in from other counties because the home field district attorney is being sued for wrongly convicting and imprisoning the defendant in the past? You can relax. Also protected under this new felony statute are *"special prosecutor[s] appointed under"* the Wisconsin statutes.[10]

But while Ken Kratz and other special prosecutors are safe, Jerry Buting, Dean Strang, and the rest of us defense lawyers are not protected under the new law. Unfortunately, we were not worthy of the legislature's efforts and are still fair game for projectile saliva.

Chapter 15

A CLOSING ARGUMENT

After a person sits through a long trial—or reads a long book—the last thing he or she wants is an extended, drawn out closing argument. So I will be brief in sharing my final thoughts—not about Avery's or Dassey's guilt or innocence, but about "the system."

Most people claim to "know" more than they can. And this human tendency toward overconfidence was on full display in *Making a Murderer*. For example, many people, including the jurors, knew that Steven Avery beat and raped Penny Beerntsen. Even today, some people in the Manitowoc Sheriff's Department still know that Avery is guilty of that crime—or at least they deny knowing that he is innocent—despite DNA evidence proving that Gregory Allen was the real perpetrator. Similarly, with regard to the Teresa Halbach case, a lot of people knew, long before the first piece of evidence was presented in court, that Avery was guilty of that crime, too.

This type of thinking is ill-suited for criminal law. Dean Strang stated in the documentary that "a chase for truth in a criminal trial can be vain."[1] And for that reason, chasing the truth is not the appropriate goal to begin with. As explained in chapter 7, the real question is whether the state has presented sufficient evidence to prove guilt beyond a reasonable doubt. But unfortunately, even Wisconsin's official jury instruction promotes the fallacy that we can somehow find, obtain, or otherwise divine the truth of what really happened. The instruction concludes by specifically telling jurors not to do their constitutionally mandated duty. The instruction tells them, "[Y]ou are *not* to search for doubt. You are to search for the *truth*."[2]

I challenge readers of this book to think of the Avery case in a different way. Stop speculating about the truth, as Wisconsin juries are erroneously instructed to do. The reality is that the Halbach murder was not video recorded, so we may never "know" where she was killed, who killed her, or why someone killed her. Some of these things might have been knowable at one time, but such knowledge could be lost to us forever thanks to the government's sole focus on Avery and its failure to even consider, let alone investigate, any other suspect or scenario for Halbach's murder. Because of this, we may never determine "the truth," no matter how long we search for it or how hard we think about it.

So instead, think about *Making a Murderer* in terms of the system we used to arrive at the convictions. And then decide whether, as a society, that system is sufficient to justify convicting Avery, Dassey, and others, and then locking them away for decades or even life.

For example, can we be confident in the outcome of Avery's trial for the Halbach murder knowing that the Manitowoc Sheriff's Department—the agency involved in wrongfully convicting him once before and on the hook for millions of dollars—was intimately involved in the investigation and collection of the evidence against him? Can we be confident in the outcome knowing that the prosecutor was allowed to use PhDs and other so-called experts to cloak his arguments in pseudoscientific certainty? Can we be confident in the outcome knowing that Wisconsin's Denny rule prevented Avery's defense team from arguing or presenting evidence that a specific third party, other than Avery or Dassey, killed Halbach? Can we be confident in the outcome knowing that, although we call our prosecutors "ministers of justice," the lawyer ethics rules are completely ineffective in constraining their pretrial conduct and their trial tactics? And finally, can we be confident that the jurors were really convinced of Avery's guilt beyond a reasonable doubt when they were instructed "not to search for doubt," and then rendered an irrational split verdict?

And with regard to Dassey, can we be confident that he raped, tortured, and killed Halbach when his confession was contradicted by the physical evidence and was obtained through interrogation tactics known to produce false confessions in timid, compliant, learning-disabled child suspects? Can we be confident in the outcome of Dassey's trial given that some of his statements—in fact, the most damning of his statements—were the result of his own defense lawyer working with the government in hopes of reaching a plea bargain rather than working against the government with the goal of winning at trial?

In sum, it really is all about the system. Admittedly, it is fun to speculate about the truth of what really happened. But while such speculation is interesting watercooler talk, and may serve to pass the time in an entertaining way, it is at best a fruitless exercise. So regardless of what you think the truth is in the Avery and Dassey cases, set that aside and ask yourself these questions. If *you* were accused of a crime in Manitowoc County, Wisconsin, would you move for a change of venue to another county if you could? And knowing that criminal law and procedure is the same throughout Wisconsin, regardless of the county, would you want to move your case out of state, to another jurisdiction, if you had that option? And even if you could move your case to another state, is that state's system plagued by some of the same problems as Wisconsin's?

If you answered yes to the above questions, then the truth is that we desperately need to rework our criminal justice system from scratch. Such reform would be too late to help Avery and Dassey, but it's not too late to help the next person who will be falsely accused of a crime.

UPDATES ON
AVERY AND DASSEY

M uch has happened in the Avery and Dassey cases since *Making a Murderer* first aired in December 2015. After losing his appeals in the Wisconsin state court system, Avery has obtained new post-conviction counsel. On August 26, 2016, attorney Kathleen Zellner filed a 154-page "Motion for Post-Conviction Scientific Testing" with the trial court in Manitowoc County. In it, she states that Steven Avery "is completely and totally innocent of the murder of Teresa Halbach. . . ." Further, "Mr. Avery has already completed a series of tests that will conclusively establish his innocence in conjunction with the additional forensic tests he is seeking in this motion."[1]

Some aspects of the lengthy motion for scientific testing will likely be opposed by the state. Assuming the court grants the motion in part or in full, the actual scientific testing could take several months. Then, as Zellner states in the motion, "All of this evidence will be presented in Mr. Avery's post-conviction petition which will be filed after the new test results are obtained from the tests requested in the instant motion."[2] The state, in turn, would likely oppose whatever relief Zellner requests in her petition, thus prolonging the litigation at this particular stage of the proceedings.

After the litigation eventually plays out at the Manitowoc County trial court, more litigation could follow in the state appellate court (again), and possibly in the state supreme court or even in the federal court system. In other words, it could be many months, or possibly even years, until Avery obtains a final resolution—one way or the other—in his case.

While Avery has real hope, Brendan Dassey has results. Like Avery, Dassey lost in his appeals in the Wisconsin state court system. However, Dassey's post-conviction counsel, Laura Nirider and Robert Dvorak, achieved success in the federal district court for the Eastern District of Wisconsin. On August 12, 2016, the federal court issued its decision in the case of *Dassey v. Dittmann* (the warden at the prison), where it addressed the issue of Dassey's coerced confession.

To recap, Dassey's state trial court judge and the Wisconsin Court of Appeals had ruled that Dassey's confession was voluntary and therefore admissible at his trial. The federal court disagreed. Despite the incredibly high standard imposed on defendants under the poorly named "Antiterrorism and Effective Death Penalty Act" (AEDPA), the federal court held that the Wisconsin Court of Appeals' decision was not "merely wrong," but, more important, "was an unreasonable application of clearly established federal law."[3]

More specifically, the federal court held that Mark Wiegert's and Tom Fassbender's "repeated false promises, when considered in conjunction with all relevant factors, most especially Dassey's age, intellectual deficits, and the absence of a supportive adult, rendered Dassey's confession involuntary under the Fifth and Fourteenth Amendments."[4]

This decision was a serious blow to the state of Wisconsin, particularly after what *Making a Murderer* has revealed about its law enforcement agents, prosecutors, and judges. As a result, the state had only two real choices: (1) "initiate . . . proceedings to retry"[5] Dassey, but without the coerced confession; or (2) appeal the federal court's ruling to the Seventh Circuit Court of Appeals. Much like Dassey did when presented with two options by Wiegert and Fassbender (see chapter 6), the state selected the lesser of two evils. It picked option number two, and appealed the federal court's decision.

Other than a handful of prosecutors and law enforcement agents working in the state of Wisconsin, few people on the planet actually believe that Dassey's confession was true, or even voluntary. If truth or voluntariness were the issues to be decided at the Seventh Circuit, Dassey would win the appeal, hands down. Instead, given the incredibly high hurdle that AEDPA imposes on state court defendants who seek relief in the federal court system, the issue will more likely come down to this: when the Wisconsin appellate court denied Dassey's appeal asking it to suppress his so-called confession, was its decision "merely wrong," or was it "*so wrong* that *no reasonable judge* could have reached that decision"?[6]

It seems odd that Dassey's entire life should hinge *not* on whether the state appellate court got it wrong, but rather the *degree* to which it got it wrong. This bizarre scenario seems more like the product of a *Twilight Zone* episode than of a modern system of criminal justice. The linguists of the whole thing—whether the appellate court was "merely wrong" or "so wrong"—reminds me of the comic strip where the trial judge, a cat, asks the defendant, a dog, whether he pleads "guilty," "really guilty," or "really, really guilty." The difference between Dassey's case and the comic strip, of course, is that the seemingly meaningless distinction in Dassey's case actually makes all the difference in the world.

Once the Seventh Circuit decides the state's appeal, the losing party will have the option of appealing to the US Supreme Court; however, that is not an appeal as a matter of right. In other words, it would be up to the US Supreme Court to decide if it wishes to accept the appeal.

While that brings us up-to-date on the Avery and Dassey cases, what about the viewers who can't get enough of *Making a Murderer*? On this front, the news is far more certain. At the time of this writing, Netflix has announced that season two is forthcoming. As a result, Wisconsin's criminal justice system will remain in the national spotlight for at least a little while longer.

ABOUT THE AUTHOR

Michael D. Cicchini is a Wisconsin criminal defense attorney. He practices in Kenosha, about two hours south of Manitowoc.

Cicchini has obtained dismissals and jury trial acquittals in dozens of cases including conspiracy to commit murder, robbery by force, sexual assault, substantial battery, child abuse, and other serious felonies. He was named a "top young lawyer" in Wisconsin by *Super Lawyers* and *Milwaukee* magazines from 2006 through 2010, and a "top 100 trial lawyer" in Wisconsin by the American Trials Lawyers Association (now the National Trial Lawyers) in 2009. He has also been named a "top criminal defense lawyer" in Wisconsin by other organizations.

In addition to practicing criminal defense, Cicchini also writes extensively on legal matters. His output includes two other books, eighteen law review articles, a monthly column at the *Wisconsin Law Journal*, and several guest posts at the *Marquette University Law School Faculty Blog*. He also writes at *The Legal Watchdog* blog, which he founded in 2010.

Cicchini earned his JD, summa cum laude and first in his class, from Marquette University Law School in Milwaukee. Before law school he earned his MBA degree and CPA certificate and worked in the corporate world.

Visit www.CicchiniLaw.com for more information, including links to his books and the full text of his law review articles.

NOTES

INTRODUCTION: WELCOME TO THE HELLMOUTH

1. Dana Reston, "Witch," *Buffy the Vampire Slayer*, season 1, episode 3, dir. Stephan Cragg, perf. Anthony Head as Rupert Giles, aired March 17, 1997 (Los Angeles: 20th Century Fox Television).

2. Mary Spicuzza, "Prosecutor Warns Teachers about New Sex Education Curriculum," *Wisconsin State Journal*, April 6, 2010, http://host .madison.com/wsj/news/local/govt_and_politics/prosecutor-warns -teachers-about-new-sex-education-curriculum/article_0e1496a2-41e1-11df -aeea-001cc4c03286.html (accessed April 28, 2016).

3. Wisconsin State Public Defender Admin., "Supreme Court of Wisconsin: No Fourth Amendment Protection for Locked, Underground Parking Garage," *On Point*, January 18, 2016, http://www.wisconsinappeals .net/on-point-by-the-wisconsin-state-public-defender/scow-no-4th -amendment-protection-for-locked-underground-parking-garage/ (accessed April 28, 2016).

4. Michael D. Cicchini, "Judge Makes up Facts and Sends Autistic Defendant to Prison," *Legal Watchdog*, November 28, 2010, http://the legalwatchdog.blogspot.com/2010/11/judge-makes-up-facts-and-sends -autistic.html (accessed April 28, 2016).

5. Michael D. Cicchini, "Sex Offender Registries: They're Not Just for Sex Offenders Anymore," *Legal Watchdog*, December 4, 2010, http:// thelegalwatchdog.blogspot.com/2010/12/sex-offender-registries-theyre -not-just.html (accessed April 28, 2016).

6. State v. Smith, 716 N.W. 2d 482, 495 (Wis. 2006). The dissent, however, had a more rational view, and believed that "an objectively reasonable person in the place of the challenged prospective juror would not ordinarily

be able to separate his or her economic and loyalty interests from the deter-
minations he or she would be required to make as juror. An employee of a
district attorney's office should therefore be struck as a juror for cause when
that office is prosecuting a case." (Abrahamson, C. J., dissenting.)

7. Michael O'Hear, "Wisconsin v. Minnesota," *Marquette Univ. Law
School Faculty Blog*, May 18, 2011, http://law.marquette.edu/faculty
blog/2011/05/18/wisconsin-v-minnesota/ (accessed April 28, 2016).

8. Moira Demos and Laura Ricciardi, *Making a Murderer*, dir. Moira
Demos and Laura Ricciardi, aired December 18, 2015 (Los Angeles:
Synthesis Films and Netflix).

9. Although not specifically discussed in the documentary, one of Avery's
appellate court decisions indicates that he presented sixteen alibi witnesses
in his defense. State v. Avery, 570 N.W.2d 573, 575 (Ct. App. Wis. 1997).

10. Although the documentary referred to the key being discovered on
the seventh search, the appellate court decided that it was discovered on the
sixth search. State v. Avery, 804 N.W.2d 216, 220 (Ct App. Wis. 2011).

11. Avery's trial court documents in the Halbach case—including the
criminal complaints, motions, briefs, jury instructions, and other filings—
can be found at http://www.stevenaverycase.org/keydocuments/. Much
of the evidence from Avery's Halbach trial—including photographs and
audio recordings—can be found at http://www.stevenaverycase.org/.
Avery's and Dassey's state-level post-conviction and appellate court
documents—including attorney briefs and court decisions—can be found
by searching the database at https://wscca.wicourts.gov/index.xsl. Finally,
cited law review articles authored or coauthored by Michael Cicchini can
be found at http://www.cicchinilawoffice.com/articles.html.

CHAPTER 1: EYEWITNESS (MIS)IDENTIFICATION

1. State v. Avery, 414 N.W.2d 319 (Ct. App. Wis. 1987); State v. Avery,
570 N.W.2d 573 (Ct. App. Wis. 1997).

2. Michael D. Cicchini and Joseph G. Easton, "Reforming the Law
on Show-Up Identifications," *Journal of Criminal Law and Criminology* 100
(2010): 381, 385–88.

3. State v. Dubose, 699 N.W.2d 582, 592 (Wis. 2005) (emphasis added).

4. Ibid., p. 584, n. 1. "A 'showup' is an out-of-court pretrial identification procedure in which a suspect is presented singly to a witness for identification purposes."

5. Moira Demos and Laura Ricciardi, *Making a Murderer*, dir. Moira Demos and Laura Ricciardi, aired December 18, 2015 (Los Angeles: Synthesis Films and Netflix). About twenty years after the event, when testifying at a deposition, Judy Dvorak denied that she had responded that way—"that sounds like Steven Avery"—but admitted that she may have made such a statement "that evening, or possibly at the sheriff's department."

6. State v. Avery, 570 N.W.2d 573, 580 (Ct. App. Wis. 1997). Avery's booking photo revealed that his eyes were not just blue, but *bright* blue.

7. About twenty years after the event, when testifying at a deposition, Gene Kusche denied drawing the sketch based on the booking photo, and insisted that he drew it based on Penny Beerntsen's description of the perpetrator. He admitted, however, that "my sketch looks more like Steven Avery than it does Gregory Allen," the real perpetrator. Demos and Ricciardi, *Making a Murderer*.

8. Jessica Lee, "Note: No Exigency, No Consent: Protecting Innocent Suspects from the Consequences of Non-Exigent Show-Ups," *Columbia Human Rights Law Review* 36 (2005): 755, 769, quoting Patrick M. Wall, *Eye-Witness Identification in Criminal Cases* (Springfield, IL: Charles C Thomas, 1965), p. 28.

9. United States v. Funches, 84 F.3d 249, 254 (7th Cir. 1996). "A show-up is inherently suggestive because the witness is likely to be influenced by the fact that the police appear to believe the person brought in is guilty, since presumably the police would not bring in someone that they did not suspect had committed the crime."

10. Stovall v. Denno, 388 U.S. 293, 302 (1967).

11. State v. Dubose, 699 N.W.2d 582 (Wis. 2005).

12. Demos and Ricciardi, *Making a Murderer*.

13. A show-up is usually conducted with a single *live* suspect, but can also take the form of a single photograph or, in Avery's case, a single sketch.

14. If a victim is certain that her attacker was, for example, Caucasian, the Caucasian suspect should not be surrounded by all African American fillers in the photo array or lineup. Such a poorly constructed identification procedure would be even more suggestive than a show-up procedure.

15. State v. Dubose, 699 N.W.2d 582, 594 (Wis. 2005). "A lineup or photo array is generally fairer than a showup, because it distributes the probability of identification among the number of persons arrayed, thus reducing the risk of a misidentification."

16. State v. Avery, 414 N.W.2d 319, *12 (Wis. Ct. App. 1987).

17. Wisconsin Office of the Attorney General, *Model Policy and Procedure for Eyewitness Identification* (Madison: Wisconsin Department of Justice, 2005), p. 6. For additional discussion, see State v. Dubose, 699 N.W.2d 582, 594 (Wis. 2005). "[I]t is important that a suspect be shown to the witness only once."

18. State v. Dubose, 699 N.W.2d 582 (Wis. 2005), quoting Foster v. California, 394 U.S. 440, 443 (1969).

19. Calvin TerBeek, "A Call for Precedential Heads: Why the Supreme Court's Eyewitness Identification Jurisprudence is Anachronistic and Out-of-Step with the Empirical Reality," *Law and Psychology Review* 31 (2007): 21, quoting Elizabeth Loftus, *Eyewitness Testimony* (Cambridge, MA: Harvard University Press, 1979), p. 19.

20. Cicchini and Easton, *Reforming the Law on Show-Up Identifications*, pp. 387–88, quoting Amy Luria, "Showup Identifications: A Comprehensive Overview of the Problems and a Discussion of Necessary Changes," *Nebraska Law Review* 86 (2008): 515, 525.

21. State v. Avery, 414 N.W.2d 319, *14 (Ct. App. Wis. 1987).

22. Lee, "No Exigency, No Consent," p. 773. More recent research suggests a moderate, positive correlation between confidence and accuracy. However, this relationship is complex. For example, comments by the police to the witness (e.g., "You got it right!") immediately after the identification procedure can artificially bolster the witness's confidence. Similarly, the lapse of time can also artificially bolster the witness's confidence, which is why his confidence level immediately after a *properly*

conducted identification procedure is probably more relevant than his confidence level by the time he eventually testifies at trial.

23. TerBeek, "A Call for Precedential Heads," p. 24.

24. Suzannah B. Gambell, "Comment: The Need to Revisit the Neil v. Biggers Factors: Suppressing Unreliable Eyewitness Identifications," *Wyoming Law Review* 6 (2006): 189, 219.

25. Keith A. Findley, "Toward a New Paradigm of Criminal Justice: How the Innocence Movement Merges Crime Control and Due Process," *Texas Tech Law Review* 41 (2008): 133.

26. State v. Dubose, 699 N.W.2d 582 (Wis. 2005).

27. State v. Nawrocki, 746 N.W.2d 509, 519 (Wis. Ct. App. 2008).

28. William J. Cromie, "False Memories: How People Remember Things That Never Happened," *Harvard University Gazette*, September 19, 1996, http://news.harvard.edu/gazette/1996/09.19/FalseMemories.html (accessed April 28, 2016); Erika Hayasaki, "The End of Eyewitness Testimonies," *Newsweek*, November 19, 2014, http://www.newsweek.com/2014/11/28/end-eyewitness-testimonies-285414.html (accessed April 28, 2016).

29. Ibid.

CHAPTER 2: NEWLY DISCOVERED EVIDENCE

1. Barry Scheck, "Symposium: Thinking Outside the Box: Proposals for Change: Closing Remarks," *Cardozo Law Review* 23 (2002): 899, 901.

2. State v. Avery, 570 N.W.2d 573, 580 (Ct. App. Wis. 1997). His actual booking photo reveals that his eyes were not just blue, but *bright* blue.

3. Ibid.

4. State v. Avery, 414 N.W.2d 319 (Ct. App. Wis. 1987).

5. Ibid., p. *14 (emphasis added).

6. Ibid., p. *15 (emphasis added).

7. State v. Avery, 570 N.W.2d 573, 580 (Ct. App. Wis. 1997).

8. Ibid., p. 575.

9. Ibid.

10. Ibid.

11. Ibid., p. 576.

12. Moira Demos and Laura Ricciardi, *Making a Murderer*, dir. Moira Demos and Laura Ricciardi, aired December 18, 2015 (Los Angeles: Synthesis Films and Netflix).

13. State v. Avery, 570 N.W.2d 573, 577 (Ct. App. Wis. 1997) (emphasis added).

14. Ibid. (emphasis added).

15. State v. Armstrong, 700 N.W.2d 98, 131 (Wis. 2005).

16. State v. Avery, 570 N.W.2d 573, 581 (Ct. App. Wis. 1997).

17. Ibid.

18. Ibid., p. 582.

19. Ibid., p. 580 (emphasis added).

20. Innocence Project: The Cases: Steven Avery, http://www .innocenceproject.org/cases-false-imprisonment/steven-avery (accessed April 28, 2016).

CHAPTER 3: SEEK, AND (EVENTUALLY) YE SHALL FIND

1. U.S. Const. amend. IV.

2. Welsh v. Wisconsin, 466 U.S. 740, 748 (1984) (emphasis added).

3. Defendant's Motion to Suppress Evidence: Franks v. Edwards Violation, Lack of Probable Cause for Warrant, and Multiple Executions of Warrant, pp. 12–19, Case No. 2005-CF-381, Manitowoc Co., Wis.

4. State v. Avery, 804 N.W.2d 216, 223-25 (Ct. App. Wis. 2011).

5. U.S. Const. amend. VI.

6. The courts, however, often get even this wrong. Wisconsin Public Defender Admin., "Conviction for Quadruple Homicide at *Questions* Bar Affirmed Despite Possible Sixth Amendment Violations," *On Point*, June 4, 2014, http://www.wisconsinappeals.net/on-point-by-the-wisconsin-state-public -defender/conviction-for-quadruple-homicide-at-questions-bar-affirmed -despite-possible-sixth-amendment-violations/ (accessed April 28, 2016).

7. What is "just," of course, is all a matter of perspective. For

example, most police searches involve drug cases. And in Wisconsin, a person growing a single marijuana plant for personal use or, under certain circumstances, merely possessing a marijuana cigarette for personal use, is guilty of a *felony*. In many of these cases, Wisconsin judges will send such defendants to jail or even prison. Given the dramatically different laws that exist in Colorado and other socially liberal states, it is certainly arguable that a defendant who uses the Fourth Amendment to escape Wisconsin's reach is, in fact, escaping an *unjust* punishment.

8. Bill Rankin, "Judge Accused of Pre-Signing Warrants, Propositioning Woman Resigns," *Atlanta Journal-Constitution*, August 16, 2012, http://www.ajc.com/news/news/local-govt-politics/judge-accused-of-pre-signing-warrants-propositioni/nRMHb/ (accessed April 28, 2016).

9. State v. Avery, 804 N.W.2d 216, 222 (Ct. App. Wis. 2011) (emphasis added).

10. Ibid., p. 223.

11. McDonald v. State, 259 S.W.2d 524, 524-25 (Tenn. 1953).

12. State v. LaCount, 750 N.W.2d 780 (Wis. 2008).

13. State v. Avery, 804 N.W.2d 216, 223 (Ct. App. Wis. 2011) (emphasis added).

14. Brief of Defendant-Appellant, pp. 9–13; 23–50, Case No. 2010AP000411, Ct. App. Wis., Dist. II.

15. Ibid., p. 34.

16. Ibid.

17. Ibid.

18. Ibid., p. 10

19. State v. Avery, 804 N.W.2d 216, 224, n 3 (Ct. App. Wis. 2011). Naming the items included in the warrant, which were limited to Halbach's remains, Halbach's personal property, forensic evidence proving that Halbach was present in the home, and any "instrumentalities capable of taking human life. . . ."

20. Ibid., p. 225. "We are satisfied that the decision [to reenter] was not only reasonable but necessary. . . ."

21. Ibid., p. 224, n. 4.

22. Ibid., p. 225, n. 5.

23. Ibid., p. 226 (emphasis added).

24. Ibid.

25. Ibid., pp. 226–27.

26. Brief of Defendant-Appellant, p. 39.

27. Ibid., p. 42.

28. State v. Avery, 804 N.W.2d 216, 227 (Ct. App. Wis. 2011).

29. Brief of Defendant-Appellant, p. 39. "[I]f the key was secreted in the bookcase as the officers surmised, it was only due to the twisting, shaking and pulling of the bookcase that the key was discovered."

30. State v. Kennedy, 396 N.W.2d 765 (Ct. App. Wis. 1986).

31. Herring v. United States, 129 S. Ct. 695, 700 (2009) (emphasis added).

CHAPTER 4: WEIRD SCIENCE

1. Frank L. H. Wolfs, "Introduction to the Scientific Method," Appendix E, http://teacher.nsrl.rochester.edu/phy_labs/appendixe/appendixe.html (accessed April 28, 2016).

2. Ibid.

3. Defendant's Statement on Planted Blood, Case No. 2005-CF-381, Manitowoc Co., Wis.

4. Moira Demos and Laura Ricciardi, *Making a Murderer*, dir. Moira Demos and Laura Ricciardi, aired December 18, 2015 (Los Angeles: Synthesis Films and Netflix).

5. Ibid.

6. Ibid.

7. Ibid.

8. Ibid.

9. Ibid.

10. Ibid.

11. This phenomenon was not only obvious in *Making a Murderer*, but has also been well documented. Saul M. Kassin, Itiel E. Dror, and Jeff Kukucka, "The Forensic Confirmation Bias: Problems, Perspectives, and

Proposed Solutions," *Journal of Applied Research in Memory and Cognition* 2 (2013): 42.

12. Demos and Ricciardi, *Making a Murderer.*

13. State v. Avery, 570 N.W.2d 573 (Ct. App. Wis. 1997).

14. Wisconsin Statutes § 907.02 (2005–06).

15. Daniel D. Blinka, "The *Daubert* Standard in Wisconsin: A Primer," *Wisconsin Lawyer*, March 2011, http://www.wisbar.org/newspublications/ wisconsinlawyer/pages/article.aspx?Volume=84&Issue=3&ArticleID=2348 (accessed April 28, 2016).

16. Wisconsin Statutes § 907.02 (2013–14).

17. Blinka, "The *Daubert* Standard."

18. Wisconsin Public Defender, Admin., "Drug Recognition Evaluator Passes *Daubert* Test for Admissibility of Expert Testimony," *On Point*, April 13, 2016 (emphasis added), http://www.wisconsinappeals.net/on-point -by-the-wisconsin-state-public-defender/drug-recognition-evaluator-passes -daubert-test-for-admissibility-of-expert-testimony/ (accessed April 28, 2016).

19. Wisconsin Public Defender, Admin., "Social Worker's Testimony about Behavior of Child Abuse Victims Passes *Daubert*," *On Point*, December 10, 2015, http://www.wisconsinappeals.net/on-point-by-the -wisconsin-state-public-defender/social-workers-testimony-about-child -abuse-victims-admissible-under-daubert/ (accessed April 28, 2016).

20. Ibid.

CHAPTER 5: THE WRONG-PERSON DEFENSE

1. Stephen Michael Everhart, "Putting a Burden of Production on the Defendant Before Admitting Evidence that Someone Else Committed the Crime Charged: Is It Constitutional?" *Nebraska Law Review* 76 (1997): 272, 293.

2. Wisconsin Criminal Jury Instructions No. 140. For a discussion of the true purpose of the criminal jury trial, see Chapter 7: Truth, Doubt, and the Burden of Proof.

3. For additional suspects in the Halbach murder, see State v. Avery,

804 N.W.2d 216, 233 (Ct. App. Wis. 2011), naming several alternative perpetrators.

4. Moira Demos and Laura Ricciardi, *Making a Murderer*, dir. Moira Demos and Laura Ricciardi, aired December 18, 2015 (Los Angeles: Synthesis Films and Netflix).

5. Holmes v. South Carolina, 547 U.S. 319, 324 (2006). "Whether rooted directly in the Due Process Clause of the Fourteenth Amendment or in the Compulsory Process or Confrontation Clauses of the Sixth Amendment, the Constitution guarantees criminal defendants a meaningful opportunity to present a complete defense."

6. State's Denny Motion Prohibiting [sic] Evidence of Third-Party Liability, Case No. 2005-CF-381, Manitowoc Co., Wis.

7. Order Regarding State's Denny Motion Prohibiting [sic] Evidence of Third-Party Liability, Case No. 2005-CF-381, Manitowoc Co., Wis.

8. State v. Denny, 357 N.W.2d 12 (Ct. App. Wis. 1984).

9. *See* Michael D. Cicchini, "An Alternative to the Wrong-Person Defense," *George Mason University Civil Rights Law Journal* 24 (2013): 1.

10. Wisconsin Criminal Jury Instructions No. 175 (emphasis added).

11. State v. Avery, 804 N.W.2d 216, 231 (Ct. App. Wis. 2011), affirming the trial court's Decision and Order on Admissibility of Third-Party Liability Evidence.

12. State v. Wilson, 864 N.W.2d 52 (Wis. 2015).

13. Ibid., p. 65.

14. Ibid. (emphasis added).

15. Ibid., p. 68.

16. Ibid., p. 69.

17. Ibid., p. 55.

18. Ibid., p. 69. When an appellate court wants to make the defendant's theory sound far-fetched or confusing, it will throw up its metaphoric arms and use the phrase "shooter or shooters," or, similarly, "killer or killers," to imply that the defendant isn't being specific or clear enough to allow him to use his chosen defense at trial.

19. State v. Avery, 570 N.W.2d 573, 581 (Ct. App. Wis. 1997)

20. Ibid.

21. Ibid., p. 582.

22. Ibid.

23. State v. Wilson, 864 N.W.2d 52, 70 (Wis. 2015). Other justifications for the near-impossible-to-satisfy Denny rule have been offered, including that allowing a defendant to point the finger at another person could confuse the jury. There are two problems with this justification. First, it begins with the assumption that the defendant is, in fact, guilty, and that the jury should not be permitted to conclude otherwise. And second, if the jury is ultimately confused about whether it was the defendant or the third party who committed the crime, that so-called confusion is nothing more than reasonable doubt. *See* Cicchini, "An Alternative to the Wrong-Person Defense," pp. 18–20.

24. State v. Avery, 804 N.W.2d 216, 232 (Ct. App. Wis. 2011), quoting Avery's trial judge.

25. Wisconsin Criminal Jury Instructions No. 140.

26. Kyles v. Whitley, 514 U.S. 419, 446 (1995). Kyles was specifically adopted in Wisconsin by State v. DelReal, 593 N.W.2d 461 (Ct. App. Wis. 1999).

27. Cicchini, "An Alternative to the Wrong-Person Defense," pp. 26–31.

28. Kyles v. Whitley, 514 U.S. 419, 442-453 (1995) (emphasis added).

29. For example, some law enforcement agents gave multiple statements about what they saw and did during the course of working Avery's cases. Their statements took different forms, including written reports, departmental communications, sworn deposition testimony in Avery's civil suit, and sworn in-court testimony in the criminal case. And sometimes, when a cop would open his mouth on a topic, the details of the story would change to meet the needs of the situation. This, in turn, led to excellent cross-examination and impeachment of these government witnesses at trial.

30. Demos and Ricciardi, *Making a Murderer*.

31. Ibid.

CHAPTER 6: INTERROGATIONS AND FALSE CONFESSIONS

1. Miranda v. Arizona, 384 U.S. 436 (1966). Although most Miranda warnings are similar, the US Supreme Court does not require any specific language in order to satisfy Miranda. In fact, there are hundreds of variations of the warnings in use across the country.

2. Anthony J. Domanico, Michael D. Cicchini, and Lawrence T. White, "Overcoming Miranda: A Content Analysis of the Miranda Portion of Police Interrogations," *Idaho Law Review* 49, no. 1 (2012): 4, quoting the version of Miranda warnings commonly used in Wisconsin.

3. State v. Dassey, 827 N.W.2d 928, *2 (Ct. App. Wis. 2013).

4. State v. Hockings, 273 N.W.2d 339 (Wis. 1979). "[B]oth custody and some form of questioning were necessary before Miranda warnings were required. . . ."

5. This allows the police to question the suspect first, without Miranda warnings, and *then* formally arrest him upon completion of the interrogation—a common law enforcement ploy designed to completely bypass Miranda. Charles D. Weisselberg, "Mourning Miranda," *California Law Review* 96 (2008): 1519, 1546.

6. State v. Dassey, 827 N.W.2d 928, *2 (Ct. App. Wis. 2013).

7. Defendant Avery's Memorandum on Brendan Dassey's Statements, p. 84, Case No. 2005-CF-381, Manitowoc Co., Wis.

8. Ibid., p. unnumbered (between pp. 85 and 86) (emphasis added).

9. Domanico, Cicchini, and White, "Overcoming Miranda," pp. 13–14.

10. Jan Hoffman, "Police Tactics Chipping Away at Suspects' Rights," *New York Times*, March 29, 1998, http://www.nytimes.com/1998/03/29/nyregion/police-tactics-chipping-away-at-suspects-rights.html.

11. Domanico, Cicchini, and White, "Overcoming Miranda," pp. 13–14.

12. Michael D. Cicchini, "The New Miranda Warning," *SMU Law Review* 65 (2012): 911, 920–21.

13. Regardless of whether the police notify a suspect of his Miranda rights, the suspect still *has* those rights. And, interestingly, a suspect's *pre*-Miranda or *pre*-arrest *silence*, though within his rights, may be used against

him in court under certain circumstances. The law on this, however, is muddied, and is well beyond the scope of this book.

14. Domanico, Cicchini, and White, "Overcoming Miranda," pp. 14–15.

15. Ibid., p. 15.

16. Defendant Avery's Memorandum on Brendan Dassey's Statements, p. 70.

17. Domanico, Cicchini, and White, "Overcoming Miranda," p. 16.

18. Ibid., pp. 15–16.

19. Ibid.

20. Ibid., p. 17.

21. Emerson Foulke and Thomas G. Sticht, "Review of Research on the Intelligibility and Comprehension of Accelerated Speech," *Psychological Bulletin* 72, no. 1 (1969): 50, 56.

22. Defendant Avery's Memorandum on Brendan Dassey's Statements, p. 108.

23. Ibid.

24. Ibid. (emphasis added).

25. Ibid. The interrogators had to ask Dassey to "speak up a little bit" when agreeing to the only option provided him: to waive, rather than invoke, his rights.

26. Saul M. Kassin, "On the Psychology of Confessions: Does Innocence Put Innocents at Risk?" *American Psychologist* 60, no. 3 (2005): 215, 219.

27. Danielle E. Chojnacki, Michael D. Cicchini, and Lawrence T. White, "An Empirical Basis for the Admission of Expert Testimony on False Confessions," *Arizona State Law Journal* 40, no. 1 (2008): 18.

28. Moira Demos and Laura Ricciardi, *Making a Murderer*, dir. Moira Demos and Laura Ricciardi, aired December 18, 2015 (Los Angeles. Synthesis Films and Netflix).

29. Ibid.

30. Defendant Avery's Memorandum on Brendan Dassey's Statements, p. 86 (emphasis added).

31. Melissa B. Russano et al., "Investigating True and False Confessions Within a Novel Experimental Paradigm," *Psychological Science* 16, no. 6 (2005): 481, 485.

32. Domanico, Cicchini, and White, "Overcoming Miranda," pp. 14–15.

33. Defendant Avery's Memorandum on Brendan Dassey's Statements, p. 3.

34. Demos and Ricciardi, *Making a Murderer.*

35. Ibid.

36. Ibid.

37. Ibid.

38. Chojnacki, Cicchini, and White, "Empirical Basis," pp. 4–5, quoting Jacqueline McMurtrie, "The Role of the Social Sciences in Preventing Wrongful Convictions," *American Criminal Law Review* 42 (2005): 1271, 1280.

39. McMurtrie, "Role of the Social Sciences," pp. 1271, 1280.

40. Richard J. Ofshe and Richard A. Leo, "The Decision to Confess Falsely: Rational Choice and Irrational Action," *Denver University Law Review* 74 (1997): 979, 984.

41. Chojnacki, Cicchini, and White, "Empirical Basis," p. 31.

42. Saul M. Kassin and Christina T. Fong, "'I'm Innocent!': Effects of Training on Judgments of Truth and Deception in the Interrogation Room," *Law and Human Behavior* 23 (1999): 499, 500–501.

43. Christian A. Meissner and Saul M. Kassin, "'He's Guilty!': Investigator Bias in Judgments of Truth and Deception," *Law and Human Behavior* 26 (2002): 469, 472.

44. Chojnacki, Cicchini, and White, "Empirical Basis," p. 32.

45. State v. Avery, 414 N.W.2d 319, *15 (Ct. App. Wis. 1987) (emphasis added).

46. Avery's mouth got him into trouble repeatedly. After Halbach went missing, he twice talked to the police *before* his arrest, talked to them again in the interrogation room *after* his arrest, and talked to the media and others while his case was pending. Some of these statements, though not admissions of guilt, were still used as evidence against him at trial.

CHAPTER 7: TRUTH, DOUBT, AND THE BURDEN OF PROOF

1. Wisconsin Criminal Jury Instructions No. 140 (2015). Avery's jurors in the Halbach murder trial also received this instruction. Jury Instructions, Case No. 2015-CF-381, Manitowoc Co., Wis.

2. This hypothetical dialogue between the would-be juror and defense lawyer is reprinted from Michael D. Cicchini, *Tried and Convicted: How Police, Prosecutors, and Judges Destroy Our Constitutional Rights* (New York: Rowman & Littlefield Publishers, 2012), p. 88.

3. Ibid., pp. 93–94 (emphasis original).

4. Transcript, Jury Trial Voir Dire Day One, p. 141, Case No. 2015-CF-381, Manitowoc Co., Wis.

5. Wisconsin Statutes § 805.08 (1).

6. Transcript, Jury Trial Voir Dire Day One, p. 151.

7. Ibid., p. 149.

8. Ibid. pp. 158–59 (emphasis added).

9. Wisconsin Criminal Jury Instructions No. 140.

10. Transcript, Jury Trial Voir Dire Day One, p. 149.

11. Defendant's Brief in Support of Wis. Stat. § 809.30(2)(h) Post-Conviction Motion, p. 2, Case No. 2005-CF-381, Manitowoc Co., Wis.

12. In Re Winship, 397 U.S. 358, 364 (1970). "[T]he Due Process Clause protects the accused against conviction except upon proof beyond a reasonable doubt. . . ."

13. Ibid., p. 362.

14. Ibid., p. 364.

15. Ibid. For a discussion of the various burdens of proof within a model of "probabilistic decision making" for "criminal guilt and punishment" see Talia Fisher, "Conviction without Conviction," *Minnesota Law Review* 96 (2012): 833.

16. Victor v. Nebraska, 511 U.S. 1, 5 (1994), giving courts tremendous leeway in their attempts to instruct jurors on the concept of reasonable doubt. For an extensive survey and discussion of the various definitions of reasonable doubt, see Richard E. Welch III, "'Give Me That Old Time Religion'": The Persistence of the *Webster* Reasonable Doubt

Instruction and the Need to Abandon It," *New England Law Review* 48 (2013): 31.

17. Arizona Criminal Jury Instructions (3d) (emphasis added).

18. Wisconsin Criminal Jury Instructions No. 140.

19. Federal Judicial Center Criminal Jury Instructions No. 21, cmt. (1987) (emphasis added); United States v. Jaramillo-Suarez, 950 F.2d 1378, 1386 (9th Cir. 1991).

20. Wisconsin Criminal Jury Instructions No. 140 (emphasis added).

21. United States v. Gonzales-Balderas, 11 F.3d 1218, 1223 (5th Cir. 1994), holding that "seek the truth" language "would be error if used in the explanation of . . . proof beyond a reasonable doubt" (emphasis added).

22. Erik R. Guenther, "What's Truth Got to Do with It? The Burden of Proof Instruction Violates the Presumption of Innocence," *Wisconsin Defender*, 2005; Michael D. Cicchini, "Criminal Court: Guilty by the Preponderance of the Evidence?" *Marquette Univ. Law School Faculty Blog*, November 16, 2010, http://law.marquette.edu/facultyblog/2010/11/16/criminal-court-guilty-by-the-preponderance-of-the-evidence/ (accessed April 28, 2016).

23. United States v. Harper, 662 F.3d 958, 961 (7th Cir. 2011). "Trials *are* searches for the truth; the burden of proof is just a device to allocate the risk of error between the parties."

24. State v. Berube, 286 P.3d 402, 411 (Ct. App. Wash. 2012).

25. Ibid; People v. Katzenberger, 178 Cal. App. 4th 1260, 1267 (2009), discussing "the jury's serious task of assessing whether the prosecution has submitted proof beyond a reasonable doubt."

26. State v. Avila, 532 N.W.2d 423, 429 (Wis. 1995). The search for the truth language, when evaluated "[i]n the context of the entire instruction," did not dilute the burden of proof.

27. Michael D. Cicchini and Lawrence T. White, "Truth or Doubt? An Empirical Test of Criminal Jury Instructions," *University of Richmond Law Review* 50 (2016): 1139.

28. Ibid., pp. 1152–56.

29. Ibid.

30. Ibid.

31. Ibid.

32. Wisconsin Criminal Jury Instructions No. 140, n. 5 explains the history of this instruction. In 1962, the instruction was worded slightly more favorably for defendants in that it repeated "reasonable doubt" at the end of the instruction, concluding, "You are to search for the truth and give the defendant the benefit of a reasonable doubt if it arises in your minds after you have carefully considered all of the evidence in the case." Then, in 1987, the instruction was revised to its current form, concluding, "While it is your duty to give the defendant the benefit of every reasonable doubt, you are not to search for doubt. You are to search for the truth."

33. United States v. Headspeth, 852 F.2d 753, 755 (4th Cir. 1988). "We have frequently admonished district courts not to attempt to define reasonable doubt in their instructions to the jury. . . ."

34. Defendant's Brief in Support of Wis. Stat. § 809.30(2)(h) Post-Conviction Motion, pp. 1–2.

35. Wisconsin Criminal Jury Instructions No. 140 (emphasis added).

CHAPTER 8: INSUFFICIENT EVIDENCE

1. State v. Ziegler, 816 N.W.2d 238, 252 (Wis. 2012) (emphasis added).

2. Defendant's Statement on Planted Blood, pp. 11–12, Case No. 2005-CF-381, Manitowoc Co., Wis. The court required Avery's defense lawyers to file this brief on their planted evidence theory. Interestingly, the blood vial was part of the public record and was easily accessible by *anyone*, including any citizen, who wanted to look at the file. Further, "the Clerk's office kept no record of those individuals who asked permission to look at the file."

3. Moira Demos and Laura Ricciardi, *Making a Murderer*, dir. Moira Demos and Laura Ricciardi, aired December 18, 2015 (Los Angeles: Synthesis Films and Netflix).

4. Ibid.

5. Ibid.

6. Defendant's Statement on Planted Blood, Case No. 2005-CF-381, Manitowoc Co., Wis.

7. Ibid., p. 19.

8. Ibid., p. 24.

9. Interestingly, because the evidence-planting defense relied more on circumstantial evidence than "direct evidence," it may have failed the Denny test for third-party liability. However, Avery's defense team was not arguing that the cops killed Halbach; rather, they were arguing that the cops framed Avery for the crime. Therefore, the proper legal test is found in *State v. Richardson*, 563 N.W.2d 899 (Wis. 1997). See Defendant's Statement on Planted Blood, pp. 1–2.

10. Demos and Ricciardi, *Making a Murderer*.

CHAPTER 9: POSTMORTEM ON PRELIMINARY HEARINGS

1. Wisconsin Statutes § 970.03.

2. State v. Williams, 544 N.W.2d 400, 403-04 (Wis. 1996).

3. One of the factors in setting cash bail is whether the defendant has been "bound over for trial after a preliminary examination. . . ." Wis. Stats. § 969.01 (4).

4. Wisconsin Statutes § 968.01.

5. Criminal Complaint, 2005-CF-381, Manitowoc Co., Wis.

6. Ibid.

7. Christine Wiseman and Michael Tobin, *Wisconsin Practice Series: Criminal Practice and Procedure*, 2nd ed. (Eagan, MN: West Publishing, 2008), § 1.12.

8. Ibid.

9. Ibid.

10. State ex rel. Cornellier v. Black, 425 N.W.2d 21, 27 (Ct. App. Wis. 1988).

11. In fairness, the state's complaint against Avery, and even the preliminary hearing, involved more factual allegations than those discussed here. However, many Wisconsin defendants have been charged

and bound over on fewer facts than those excerpted for purposes of this chapter. Therefore, for brevity, and for the purpose of making the relevant points, this chapter will focus on the evidence concerning Halbach's car key, including how and where it was found.

12. Moira Demos and Laura Ricciardi, *Making a Murderer*, dir. Moira Demos and Laura Ricciardi, aired December 18, 2015 (Los Angeles: Synthesis Films and Netflix).

13. Wisconsin Statutes. § 970.04. "If a preliminary examination has been had and the defendant has been discharged, the district attorney may file another complaint. . . ."

14. Wisconsin Statutes § 970.03 (1).

15. State ex rel. Brill v. Spieker, 72 NW.2d 906 (Wis. 1955).

16. State v. Garrity, 469 N.W.2d 219 (Wis. Ct. App. 1991).

17. Wiseman and Tobin, *Criminal Practice and Procedure*, § 8.3.

18. State ex rel. Funmaker v. Klamm, 317 N.W.2d 458, 460-61 (Wis. 1982).

19. Wiseman and Tobin, *Criminal Practice and Procedure,* § 8.42.

20. State v. Berby, 260 N.W.2d 798, 803 (Wis. 1978), holding that the preliminary hearing judge properly "relied partially on Berby's lack of *motive* in finding a lack of *probable cause*. . . ."

21. Wisconsin Statutes § 970.038.

22. There is currently a debate as to whether multiple levels of hearsay should be permitted at Wisconsin preliminary hearings. Some judges will permit only one level of hearsay; others will consider multiple levels of hearsay to bind a defendant over—even when the witnesses are unable to identify the original declarant, i.e., the person to whom the hearsay is attributable.

23. Wisconsin Statutes § 970.03 (5). "The defendant may cross-examine witnesses against the defendant, and may call witnesses on the defendant's own behalf who then are subject to cross-examination."

24. State v. O'Brien, 850 N.W.2d 8 (Wis. 2014), denying the defendant the statutory right to call the alleged victim as a witness because the defendant could not first prove, *before* putting the witness on the stand, that the testimony would be relevant for purposes of probable cause.

25. Defendant's Motion to Dismiss or Conduct Preliminary Hearing, 2005-CF-381, Manitowoc Co., Wis.

26. Order Denying Defendant's Motion to Dismiss Complaint or Conduct Preliminary Hearing, 2005-CF-381, Manitowoc Co., Wis.

27. Worse yet, and quite bizarrely, the judge doesn't even have to disclose—and in fact is discouraged from disclosing—the particular felony for which he found probable cause. Wittke v. State ex rel. Smith, 259 N.W.2d 515 (Wis. 1977).

28. State's Motion to Amend Criminal Complaint and Criminal Information, 2005-CF-381, Manitowoc Co., Wis.

29. Bailey v. State, 222 N.W.2d 871, 876 (Wis. 1974).

30. Avery's new, tacked-on charges were based on Brendan Dassey's statements that were extracted from him over the course of multiple interrogations. Under the probable cause standard, Dassey arguably should not have been considered a traditional citizen informant. Rather, Dassey was a suspect-turned-codefendant and was subjected to the coercive power of law enforcement. For purposes of a criminal complaint, therefore, his statements should not have been afforded the same presumption of truthfulness as those of a true citizen informant. State v. Paszek, 184 N.W.2d 836 (Wis. 1971), discussing the "unreliability" of certain classes of witnesses such as police informants who, much like codefendants, are expecting concessions for their statements.

31. Defendant's Motion to Dismiss Sexual Assault, Kidnapping, and False Imprisonment Charges, 2005-CF-381, Manitowoc Co., Wis.

32. Defendant's Motion for New Trial, pp. 5–13, 2005-CF-381, Manitowoc Co., Wis.

33. Ibid., pp. 1–2.

34. Ibid., p. 3, citing Sharp v. Case Corp., 595 N.W.2d 380, 388 (Wis. 1999). The civil court will review a split "jury verdict to determine whether it is fatally inconsistent. . . ."

35. Wisconsin Statutes § 970.02 (1) (c).

36. Wisconsin Statutes § 970.02 (4).

37. See Wiseman and Tobin, *Criminal Practice and Procedure,* § 8.32, discussing the benefits of waiving a preliminary hearing, including

preventing the prosecutor "preserving" a witness's testimony for later use at trial in the event the witness disappears or becomes uncooperative. Whether such testimony could be used at a later trial implicates the confrontation clause, and may hinge on whether the defendant had the opportunity for full cross-examination of the witness at the preliminary hearing—a complicated issue beyond the scope of this book.

38. State v. Burke, 451 N.W.2d 739, 742-43 (Wis. 1990).

39. State v. Cotton, 668 N.W.2d 346, 350 (Ct. App. Wis. 2003) (emphasis added).

40. This still leaves us with this question: with no evidence having been adduced at a preliminary hearing (because the preliminary hearing was waived), to what, then, are the new charges transactionally related? Most judges assume that a transactional relation to something in the criminal complaint is sufficient. This interpretation, however, would give felony defendants fewer protections than misdemeanor defendants— something that is clearly not legally proper and was never intended by the legislature.

CHAPTER 10: BAIL OR JAIL?

1. Jason Stein and Patrick Marley, "Republican Lawmakers May Try to Resurrect Bail Bonding," *Milwaukee Journal Sentinel,* May 18, 2013, http://www.jsonline.com/news/statepolitics/republican-lawmakers-may -try-to-resurrect-bail-bonding-k19vhej-208017101.html (accessed April 29, 2016).

2. Defendant's Motion to Modify Bail, 2005 CF 381, Manitowoc Co., Wis.

3. Wisconsin Statutes § 969.01 (4).

4. Wisconsin Statutes § 969.01 (1) (emphasis added).

5. Wisconsin Statutes § 969.01 (4) (emphasis added).

6. Ibid.

7. Defendant's Motion to Modify Bail (emphasis added).

8. See Daniel Massey, "City Pays Big Price for Minor Crimes," *Crain's*

New York Business, December 3, 2010, http://www.crainsnewyork.com/
article/20101203/FREE/101209955/report-city-pays-big-price-for-minor
-crimes (accessed April 29, 2016).

9. Wisconsin does have a speedy trial statute. However, the deadlines
are often disregarded, as the statute allows for continuances in the judge's
discretion. Wis. Stats. § 971.10. Other speedy trial protections, including
the constitutional right to a speedy trial, are rarely triggered in state cases,
even after a delay of several years. Barker v. Wingo, 407 U.S. 514 (1972).

10. Defendant's Motion to Modify Bail.

11. Moira Demos and Laura Ricciardi, *Making a Murderer*, dir. Moira
Demos and Laura Ricciardi, aired December 18, 2015 (Los Angeles:
Synthesis Films and Netflix).

12. Wisconsin Statutes Ch. 969.

13. Wisconsin Statutes § 946.49.

14. Daniel E. Chojnacki, Michael D. Cicchini, and Lawrence T. White,
"An Empirical Basis for the Admission of Expert Testimony on False
Confessions," *Arizona State Law Journal* 40, no. 1 (2008): 17.

15. Defendant's Memorandum Supporting Exclusion of Jail
Statements and Tapes, p. 3, 2015-CF-381, Manitowoc Co., Wis.

16. Demos and Ricciardi, *Making a Murderer*.

17. State v. Avery, 414 N.W.2d 319, *15 (Ct. App. Wis. 1987).

18. Defendant's Motion to Modify Bail.

19. Defendant's Notice Concerning Interference with Right to
Counsel, 2005-CF-381, Manitowoc Co., Wis.

20. Ibid.

21. Ibid.

22. Wisconsin Statutes §969.01 (4).

23. Ibid.

CHAPTER 11: INTRODUCTION TO LEGAL ETHICS

1. This phrase reflects the general disregard for ethics rules not
only in the legal system, but in other professions as well. For an example,
see Max Brantley, "Ethics, Schmethics: Legislators Keep Junketing,"

March 27, 2016, *Arkansas Blog*, http://www.arktimes.com/ArkansasBlog/
archives/2016/03/27/ethics-schmethics-legislators-keep-junketing
(accessed April 29, 2016).

2. Supreme Court Rules (SCR): Chapter 20, https://www.wicourts
.gov/supreme/sc_rules.jsp (accessed April 29, 2016).

3. SCR 1.9 (c).

4. Ibid.

5. Michael D. Cicchini, "On the Absurdity of Model Rule 1.9,"
Vermont Law Review 40 (2015): 69.

6. In the Matter of the Petition of Michael D. Cicchini and Terry W.
Rose to Modify SCR 20:1.9 (c) [15-04], Wisconsin Court System: Supreme
Court Rules: Pending Petitions, https://www.wicourts.gov/scrules/1504
.htm (accessed April 29, 2016).

CHAPTER 12: THE EFFECTIVE ASSISTANCE OF COUNSEL

1. Supreme Court Rules (SCR): Chapter 20: Preamble: A Lawyer's
Responsibilities, ¶ 2, https://www.wicourts.gov/supreme/sc_rules.jsp
(accessed April 29, 2016).

2. SCR 1.3, ABA cmt., ¶ 1.

3. SCR 1.1.

4. SCR 1.4.

5. SCR 1.6.

6. This two-part test is cited in nearly every Wisconsin appellate and
supreme court case dealing with a defendant's "ineffective assistance of
counsel" claim, and is based on Strickland v. Washington, 466 U.S. 668
(1984). See, e.g., State v. Johnson, 449 N.W.2d 845 (Wis. 1990).

7. Ibid.

8. State v. Dassey, 827 N.W.2d 928, ¶ 8–9 (Ct. App. Wis. 2013).

9. Ibid., ¶ 9.

10. Ibid., ¶ 11.

11. Brief of Defendant-Appellant, pp. 29–40, Case No.
2010AP3105CR, Court App. Wis., Dist. 2.

12. Although not revealed in *Making a Murderer*, "O'Kelly told Dassey that his *inconclusive* polygraph results showed a ninety-eight percent probability of deception." State v. Dassey, 827 N.W.2d 928, ¶ 10, n. 2 (Ct. App. Wis. 2013) (emphasis added).

13. Moira Demos and Laura Ricciardi, *Making a Murderer*, dir. Moira Demos and Laura Ricciardi, aired December 18, 2015 (Los Angeles: Synthesis Films and Netflix).

14. State v. Dassey, 827 N.W.2d 928, ¶ 11 (Ct. App. Wis. 2013).

15. Brief of Defendant-Appellant, p. 40 (emphasis added).

16. Ibid. (emphasis added).

17. Ibid. at 36 (emphasis added).

18. State v. Dassey, 827 N.W.2d 928, ¶ 11 (Ct. App. Wis. 2013).

19. Ibid.

20. As explained in the postscript, the federal district court reversed Dassey's conviction, but the state of Wisconsin has appealed the case to the federal appellate court for the Seventh Circuit.

21. State v. Dassey, 827 N.W.2d 928, ¶ 11 (Ct. App. Wis. 2013).

22. Office of Lawyer Regulation v. Kenneth Kratz, 851 N.W.2d 219, 222-23 (Wis. 2014).

23. For a discussion of the political nature of state bar associations, see Mauricio R. Hernandez, "Tamales and State Bars," *Irreverent Lawyer*, November 21, 2015, discussing the inherent conflict in "mandatory bar associations [that] claim to be both public protection regulators and trade associations for lawyer interests," https://lawmrh.wordpress.com/2015/11/21/tamales-and-state-bars/ (accessed April 29, 2016); David Cameron Carr, "The Great Public Protection Perpetual Motion Machine," *Kafkaesq*, January 11, 2014. "It is politically incorrect now to suggest that the State Bar do something that might only benefit its members." https://kafkaesq.com/2014/01/11/the-great-public-protection-perpetual-motion-machine/ (April 29, 2016).

CHAPTER 13: THE MINISTER OF JUSTICE

1. When I first started practicing criminal defense, Wisconsin was moving to its draconian "truth in sentencing" law. At a continuing legal education seminar about the law change, one of the truth-in-sentencing committee members told the attendees that, because there were so many different crimes (not all of which were located in the criminal code), they could not guarantee that they had located all of them during the course of their reclassification of crimes and penalties.

2. Wisconsin Supreme Court Rules (SCR) 3.8, ABA cmt., ¶ 1.

3. SCR 3.6 (b).

4. SCR 3.8 (f).

5. For the dates and details of the government's "media tour," see Defendant's Memorandum Supporting Motion to Dismiss, 2005-CF-381, Manitowoc Co., Wis.

6. Moira Demos and Laura Ricciardi, *Making a Murderer*, dir. Moira Demos and Laura Ricciardi, aired December 18, 2015 (Los Angeles: Synthesis Films and Netflix).

7. Ibid.

8. Ibid.

9. Ibid.

10. Ibid.

11. State's Response to Defendant's Motion to Dismiss (Pretrial Publicity), Case No. 2005-CF-381, Manitowoc Co., Wis.

12. SCR 20:3.6 (d).

13. State v. Avery, 414 N.W.2d 319, *15 (Ct. App. Wis. 1987), upholding Avery's conviction in part because Beerntsen's "identification of Avery was corroborated by Avery's statements at the time of his arrest."

14. The documentary revealed that, at a minimum, Avery talked to Colborn before his arrest and to interrogators after his arrest. He even let the sheriffs search his property, twice, before they ever got a search warrant.

15. Douglass J. Soccio, *Archetypes of Wisdom: An Introduction to Philosophy*, 8th ed. (Boston, MA: Wadsworth Cengage Learning, 2010), pp. 74–75 (emphasis added).

16. Demos and Ricciardi, *Making a Murderer*.

17. Ibid.

18. Wisconsin Criminal Jury Instructions No. 140.

19. Office of Lawyer Regulation v. Kenneth Kratz, 851 N.W.2d 219, 222–23 (Wis. 2014).

20. Ibid., p. 220.

21. Ibid., p. 224.

CHAPTER 14: THE POLITICS OF LEGAL REFORM

1. Wisconsin Criminal Jury Instructions No. 140 (emphasis added).

2. Michael D. Cicchini and Lawrence T. White, "Truth or Doubt? An Empirical Test of Criminal Jury Instructions," *University of Richmond Law Review* 50 (2016): 1139.

3. Michael D. Cicchini, "An Alternative to the Wrong-Person Defense," *George Mason University Civil Rights Law Journal* 24 (2013): 1, 23–25. Citations and footnotes within the article have *not* been reproduced in this excerpt. For the full article, including original citations and footnotes, visit the articles page of www.CicchiniLaw.com.

4. Anthony J. Domanico, Michael D. Cicchini, and Lawrence T. White, "Overcoming Miranda: A Content Analysis of the Miranda Portion of Police Interrogations," *Idaho Law Review* 49, no. 1 (2010): 18–21. Citations and footnotes within the article have *not* been reproduced in this excerpt. For the full article, including original citations and footnotes, visit the articles page of www.CicchiniLaw.com.

5. Moira Demos and Laura Ricciardi, *Making a Murderer*, dir. Moira Demos and Laura Ricciardi, aired December 18, 2015 (Los Angeles: Synthesis Films and Netflix).

6. Ibid.

7. Ibid.

8. Wisconsin Statutes § 941.375.

9. 2015 Assembly Bill 357, https://docs.legis.wisconsin.gov/2015/related/proposals/ab357.pdf (accessed May 1, 2016).

10. Ibid. (emphasis added).

CHAPTER 15: A CLOSING ARGUMENT

1. Moira Demos and Laura Ricciardi, *Making a Murderer*, dir. Moira Demos and Laura Ricciardi, aired December 18, 2015 (Los Angeles: Synthesis Films and Netflix).

2. Wisconsin Criminal Jury Instructions No. 140 (emphasis added).

POSTSCRIPT: UPDATES ON AVERY AND DASSEY

1. Defendant's Motion for Post-Conviction Scientific Testing, 2005-CF-381, Manitowoc Co., Wis.

2. Ibid.

3. Dassey v. Dittmann, 2016 U.S. Dist. LEXIS 106971, *110.

4. Ibid.

5. Ibid., p. *111.

6. Ibid., p. *57.